RADICAL OUTREACH

The Recovery of Apostolic Ministry and Evangelism

George G. Hunter III

Abingdon Press
Nashville

RADICAL OUTREACH
THE RECOVERY OF APOSTOLIC MINISTRY AND EVANGELISM

Copyright © 2003 by Abingdon Press

This book is printed on recycled, acid-free, elemental-chlorine–free paper.

Library of Congress Cataloging in Publication Data

Hunter, George G.
  Radical outreach : the recovery of apostolic ministry and evangelism / George G. Hunter III.
    p.   cm.
Includes bibliographical references (p.   ) and index.
  ISBN 068707441X
  1. Evangelistic work.   I. Title.

BV3790.H892 2003
269′ .2—dc21   2002155982

ISBN 13: 978-0-687-07441-9

All scripture quotations unless noted otherwise are taken from the New Revised Standard Version of the Bible, copyright © 1989, Division of Christian Education of the National Council of the Churches of Christ in the United States of America. Used by permission. All rights reserved.

Scripture quotations noted KJV are from the King James or Authorized Version of the Bible.

Excerpts from *Church for the Unchurched* by George G. Hunter III © 1996 Abingdon Press. Used by permission.

08 09 10 11 12—10 9 8 7 6 5

MANUFACTURED IN THE UNITED STATES OF AMERICA

*To Lyle Schaller, America's
church consultant, who once
observed that "the only
thing we know for sure about the future
is that it will surprise us," who has
taught us more about what makes
churches effective than anyone else*

And

*To Trevor Rowe, British Methodist leader, who
once asked, "What would Saint Augustine do?"
who modeled a powerful way to reflect upon
Christianity's past to inform its future*

Contents

Chapter Three: Apostolic Ministry Through "Cultural Relevance" 67

Chapter Four: Apostolic Ministry Through an Empowered Laity 97

Foreword

Radical Outreach is a must read for those who care deeply about the mission of the church in America. But it is a risky read. True, it is written in Dr. George Hunter's inimitably cogent and captivating style, full of broad awareness of the grassroots reality of the church in America, and buttressed by careful research and impressive erudition. But *Radical Outreach* may prove to be as troubling as it is informative, as disturbingly counterintuitive as it is biblically grounded and inescapably convincing. It calls for action.

The truth is, most of us don't take kindly to challenges as to how we do church. Take the charge that 80 percent of the 360,000 churches in America are stagnant or declining, and most of the remainder grow mainly by shuffling believers from one congregation to another. Hunter makes embarrassingly clear that when it comes to the call of Jesus to be "fishers for men and women," most of our congregations are content to wait for the "fish" to find us and then clamber over the gunwales of the good ship *ecclesia* in order to get in. He estimates that less than 1 percent of churches grow substantially by "conversion growth" as people come to Christ out of the unbelieving majority. Only these churches can properly be described as "apostolic" in Hunter terms. These are the congregations responding to our Lord's commission with an outward-looking missional focus that moves beyond a sedentary and member-centered "chaplaincy" to intentional "apostolicity."

The sad truth is that most churches seem to have written off great segments of the American market for mission. Few seem serious, let along "radical," about engaging those most needing the hope and healing the gospel affords: the hard-to-reach secular population, the "impossible people," the addicted, troubled, problem people to whom Jesus delighted to reach out. "It's the sick who need a physician," Jesus once said, "not the well." In all honesty, our self-serving congregations are not much enamored of Jesus' program for bringing in the "lame, the halt and the blind" to sit with proper folk at table. Hunter frames the situation with a few sharply crafted questions: Do we want to know them? Are we willing to go where they are? To spend time with them? Do we want them in our churches? And most difficult of all: Are we willing for our church to become their church too? The answers to these probing queries may well be disconcerting to comfortable traditional congregations.

The author knows that to get serious about outreach will require speaking a language understood by those we want to engage for God. Indeed, it means communicating understandably in all those nonverbal ways we "speak" to one another. That is hard work. And painful, too. It means entering into the cultural world of the other. Possibly an unknown and even frightening or offensive world. It was into just such a world that the pure Son of God was born in order to move into our neighborhood.

Dr. Hunter combs through the history of major forward

movements in evangelism and mission, surfacing the common marks of radical outreach: the early apostolic advance, the Celtic mission, the Wesleyans, and the Pentecostals. William and Catherine Booth, founders of The Salvation Army, were aflame with an apostolic passion to reach the least and the lost, the poor and the powerless. "Go for souls and go for the worst!" was his watchword. Proper congregants of their time were not greatly supportive of the Army's penchant for dragging the sewers of society to make converts. But the mission endures. After more than 135 years, subsequent generations of Salvationists, like believers of other communions, have gentrified considerably. Meanwhile, volunteer programs of service to problem populations, as they have developed into 24/7 year-round commitments, beyond the ability of volunteers alone to sustain, have tended to become professionalized and distanced from the heartbeat of the community of faith that gave them birth. As these programs diversify and bridge out into the community of human need, constant care is required to ensure that they effectively bridge back into the community of faith and its offer of grace through the gospel. For service ministries to prove evangelistically effective they must be seen to flow out of the life and love of the people of God. There is always a tendency to more or less "out-source" the mission. Churches, like those Dr. Hunter profiles, which are catching the vision for engaging human and social pathologies in the name and power of Christ, may want to reference the Army's experience in this regard. The Salvation Army as much as anyone recognizes the need to renew its commitment to "radical outreach" in every generation.

Radical Outreach pulses with a passion for the recovery of apostolic priorities in mission. Its insights are illuminating. The chapter on addiction alone is worth the price of the book. Its counsel on how to break out of the "cultural islands" our churches become, enabling seekers to surmount what the author elsewhere calls the "culture barrier," is invaluable. The biblical foundations for his theses are sound. But it is not comfortable reading for the spiritually lethargic. It is not meant to be. *Radical Evangelism* is Jesus-serious about evangelism.

Paul A. Rader, General (Ret.)
former international leader
The Salvation Army
President, Asbury College
Wilmore, Kentucky

Preface

As a teacher and writer in evangelism and mission for the School of World Mission and Evangelism at Asbury Theological Seminary, I have used the term "apostolic ministry" (and related terms) for many years. In *To Spread the Power: Church Growth in the Wesleyan Spirit*, I unpacked the Church Growth strategies that can enable local churches to approach their local mission with "apostolic confidence."

In *How to Reach Secular People*, I suggested that, due to the "secularization" of the West and the growing numbers of "secular people" (with no Christian memory) who now populate every community, North America and Europe have become "mission fields" once again; our churches, therefore, now face a new "apostolic challenge." The book profiles the kind of "apostolic Christians" who reach secular people, develops additional strategies for reaching them, and profiles the kind of "apostolic congregation" that reaches secular people in terms of two focused questions: (1) What do these churches *know* that other churches do not know? (2) What do these churches *do* that other churches do not do?

Church for the Unchurched expanded upon what can now be known about the apostolic congregations that began emerging in the 1970s, which, in contrast to the traditional churches down the street, do reach secular people in significant numbers.

The Celtic Way of Evangelism tells the story of the fifth- to ninth-century "Celtic" Christian movement's essential recovery of Christianity's "apostolic mission," with insights from that ancient movement for reaching "secular postmodern" people today.

These four books refer to apostolic ministry, but they focus more upon every church's apostolic context and upon the kinds of apostolic Christians, churches, and approaches that gather the "harvest."

One day, I was perusing the new curriculum for the Master of Divinity program at Asbury's school of theology. I noticed that the program would now require a three-hour course in "Apostolic Ministry!" I contacted the theology school dean, Joel Green, and asked, "Where did you get that? What do I need to read to learn more about 'apostolic ministry'?" Joel replied that David Thompson and his curriculum committee said that they got the term from me, and they hoped that I would write the book about it!

This is the book! It is not the last word on the subject— more like a first word—but more than enough for any church to reach many people. I hope to produce a future book on the range of "outreach ministries," through which contemporary apostolic congregations reach people, and another book on apostolic approaches to doing evangelism. This book trumpets and delineates two indispensable themes: (1) We reach lost people who have not yet found "the way" by getting in ministry with them, and then in conversation, *not* through preaching, or witnessing, alone. (2) Apostolic movements are typically catalyzed by reaching some people thought to be unreachable, even "hopeless." This project stands in sympathy with the famous words of Saint Francis of Assisi: "Preach the Gospel at all times; when necessary, use words." Since it *is* often "necessary" to use words, the last chapter engages this perennial challenge.

Readers of my earlier books, especially *The Celtic Way of Evangelism*, will know that I like to approach Christianity's contemporary challenge historically. I am not a "real card-carrying historian," but a communication theorist and missiologist who works with historical materials. In my defense, I regard history as too important to leave to the technical historians who are obsessed with whatever happened to the Jebusites! Those of us who raise the apostolic questions cannot wait for the historians to do our homework for us.

People occasionally ask how this project relates to earlier projects and movements that aimed to recover and restore early, "primitive," or ancient apostolic Christianity. The reader will note my strong affinity for past movements, such as the Celtic movement and the Wesleyan movement, that meant to recover Christianity's earlier mission (and message). The reader may also discern, from silence, my lack of interest in issues such as whether churches should worship on Saturday or Sunday and whether churches should, or should not, use musical instruments; I leave all such issues to others.

People more than occasionally ask how my approach relates to the writing of C. Peter Wagner and others on (what they call) the "new apostolic church" movement. A brief answer can be stated in three words: "With some difficulty!" Three comments will suggest why.

1. In the mid-1990s, Pete Wagner was speaking, writing, and hosting conferences on "postdenominational" churches; he featured a number of growing independent and charismatic churches across the country and beyond.

In 1996, my book *Church for the Unchurched*, in which I feature nine "apostolic congregations," was published. Pete telephoned me one day, asking, "Do you have proprietary rights on the term 'apostolic'?" I remember reflecting that, since the term predates me by nineteen centuries, it had not even occurred to me to claim propriety rights! At that moment, it seems, Pete jacked up his car, removed "postdenominational," and ran the term "apostolic" underneath![1] Undoubtedly, he liked the term "apostolic" more than "postdenominational"; so do I.

I have no reasons, however, to regard the two terms as synonymous, or particularly interchangeable. As this book explains, apostolic congregations believe themselves to be "sent" to reach one or more "pre-Christian" populations, and their effectiveness is indicated (Church growth missiologists would say) by their "conversion growth" rate. Many apostolic congregations are denominational churches; many of the postdenominational churches grow much more by biological growth and (especially) transfer growth than by conversion growth.

2. The new apostolic church movement rightly regards visionary church leadership as necessary for great Christian movements, and the ways that their leaders "network" and form "alliances" may well be more effective than traditional denominational structures; my difference is one of addition. In *Leading and Managing a Growing Church*, I demonstrate, from the Scriptures, that both leadership *and* "management" (defined as "getting things done through other people") are indispensable for Christian movements. My real problem with the movement's leadership theme is with two excesses.

First, I cannot support the movement's obsession to restore the "office of Apostle" for today's Church. This emphasis leaves me anxious, in part, because many of the movement's churches hand out "Apostle" as a *title*! Such interest in (really) big titles is not unprecedented. For instance, in 1789, John Wesley was peeved when Francis Asbury and Thomas Coke—his designated "superinten-dents" for the Methodist work in America—allowed them-selves to be called bishops. Today, the pastoral leaders of many churches go by much more pretentious titles, titles that embarrass their predecessors in heaven and scandalize the Church on earth with many of its publics.

So this is the time to recall that Jesus and all of the origi-nal Apostles went by their first names; that biblical prece-dent is, presumably, good enough for church leaders today. This book contends that, in any "mission field," pastors are called to an apostolic role (rather than to a chaplaincy role). Since the time of the original Apostles, the term has contin-ued as an adjective—a priest is ordained in "apostolic suc-cession," Patrick was assigned to Ireland as an "apostolic bishop," the Dominicans were established as an "apostolic order"—but there have been no more "Apostles."

Second, I cannot support the movement's implied defi-nition of an apostle as a leader who exercises command authority over one or more churches. In the history reflected in the New Testament, the apostles exercised not command authority, but moral persuasion. Paul's approach to the churches, for instance, is modeled in Ephesians 4:1—"I therefore, the prisoner in the Lord, beg you to lead a life worthy of the calling to which you have been called." Considered together, the pushes for titles and command authority are much more characteristic of the early medieval Eastern Orthodox and Roman Catholic churches than of the first-century churches founded by the Apostles. More and more Roman Catholics, at least, see the need to get over "hierarchy." There are no good reasons for Protestants to join a parade that should disband!

3. I have profound sympathy for the new apostolic church movement's stress upon prayer, healing, deliver-ance, and miracles, and even "signs and wonders" (though I have no reasons to adopt its speculations about

"territorial spirits" or its exercises in "territorial mapping"). This book positions "recovery ministries" for addictive people in rough continuity with the early church's ministries to deliver possessed people from evil spirits, and this book features the profoundly changed life as the greatest of the signs, wonders, and miracles.

This book proposes the "apostolic renewal" of tens of thousands of churches across North America and calls, as Wallace Fisher did a generation ago, traditional churches to move "from tradition to mission." In several chapters, "Old East Side Church" is my foil for exposing the pathology of "traditionalism" and for showing traditionalist churches a more apostolic way. Old East Side Church is a fiction, so any similarity between it and any specific church is purely coincidental. Old East Side Church, however, is an informed composite fiction, so any similarity between it and, say, eight of ten churches across North America is purely intentional!

I am prodding Old East Side Church because people who do not know the grace, love, and reign of God, who have never experienced justification or second birth, who are not yet following Jesus Christ and seeking his will for their lives, are lost, like sheep without a shepherd; and they need to be found, which is supposed to be Old East Side's main business. As William Temple once observed: "The true Church is the only society on earth that exists for its nonmembers."

When Old East Side's leaders do (occasionally) talk about the need to "reach out," their vision is restricted. They talk about reaching out to Old East Side's inactive members or to the people who are already visiting the church. *If* they ever consider reaching strangers, they only target people like themselves.

This book challenges Old East Siders to reach out farther—to three categories of populations. The first population is the growing number of pre-Christian secular people who have no Christian background, memory, or vocabulary, and no church to "return" to. My book *How to Reach*

Secular People especially addresses this opportunity to reach secular peoples. The second population includes those whom the "establishment church" assumes to be hopeless and incapable of becoming real Christians. The third population reflects the recent pattern of immigration to North America and consists of many urban peoples whose heart languages are not English and whose cultures are beyond Old East Side's current range of understanding.

As Jesus calls his first disciples (in John 4:35), Old East Side's leaders need to lift up their eyes and see where the fields are white for the harvest because, in many communities, these three populations constitute most of the harvest; they are "looking for Life, but in all the wrong places." This book is written with the confidence that Old East Side Church has been "brought to the Kingdom for such a time as this" and that, in measurable time, Old East Side will reach people it once never thought of reaching and will experience the power, miracles, and contagion it once assumed were no longer available.

I could acknowledge the contributions of many more people than any preface has space for, but I must acknowledge the following colleagues. Dr. Reg Johnson, my faculty colleague at Asbury, provided the case study that concludes chapter 2. Chapter 4 is indebted to two recovery specialists—Dr. George Ross, an adjunct professor at Asbury Theological Seminary, and Dr. John MacDougall, a staff pastor at Hazelden Foundation. I also thank pastors Debbie McLeod and Dick Wills of Christ United Methodist Church in Ft. Lauderdale, and pastor Steve Hoffman of Fulford United Methodist Church in North Miami Beach, for insights and entry into their recovery ministries. Chapter 6 is devoted to a case study of a single church that began practicing "radical outreach" before we knew what to call it. Pastor Charles Roesel, a dozen people on his staff, and many lay volunteers who lead the church's outreach ministries made it possible to dramatize most of the book's driving themes from this one church.

CHAPTER ONE

Western Christianity's "Corinthian" Future

Two islands, Big Diomede and Little Diomede, lie in the Bering Straight, off the coast of Alaska. The view from an airplane shows the two islands side by side, two and a half miles apart. The significant differences between the two islands are not obvious to the eye: Big Diomede belongs to Russia, and Little Diomede belongs to the U.S.A. Furthermore, the International Date Line runs between them, which makes Little Diomede unique. If you stand on Little Diomede's western shore and look West toward the bigger island, on a clear day, you can see tomorrow!

In the Western world today, we can see tomorrow, and, for students of the Scriptures, the future looks familiar. In the words of Yogi Berra, "It's déjà vu all over again." Specifically, we face a "Corinthian future"; our emerging challenge is reminiscent of the church's challenge in the ancient city of Corinth—the setting for much of Paul's ministry and correspondence in the third quarter of the first century.

This suggestion may strike the reader as an unwarranted stretch because many differences between our world and the ancient Mediterranean world will flood any reflective mind. First-century Corinth predated, by more than a thousand years, the invention of the printing press, the rise of empirical science, and the development of universities. The radio, the phonograph, and the Model T Ford would have seemed like miracles. Even the most affluent people in first-century Corinth could not "stay connected" by E-mail or cell phone, get liposuctions, or blow-dry their hair. Nevertheless, two parallels between ancient Corinth and our emerging future will so profoundly affect Christianity's future that churches whose leaders do not take these parallels seriously may have no future worth having.

An Urban Society, with Many Cultures

The early Christian movement engaged the cities of the Roman Empire; Christianity was an urban religious movement for three centuries.[1] The Messianic movement grew initially in cities—such as in Jerusalem and Antioch. Rome's persecution of the young faith scattered its disciples to the other cities of the empire. Luke's itineraries for Paul's three missionary journeys record Paul planting, or catalyzing, the Christian movement from city to city. Paul's letters are to urban churches in Rome, Galatia, Ephesus, Philippi, Colossi, Thessalonica, and Corinth. Corinth was an extensive city of about 700,000 people when Paul first engaged its people in A.D. 51.

Although most of the people in ancient Corinth could speak enough Greek to engage in trade, they spoke many different languages in their homes and represented many distinct cultures. Greeks, Italians, Jews, Egyptians, and Syrians were present in significant numbers, with other Arabic, Asian, and European peoples; and they brought their religions with them. Archaeologists have identified the ruins of at least twelve temples that were probably there in Paul's time, probably including the temples of Apollo and Aphrodite. Corinth, a major port city and the capital of the province Achaea, was a thriving center of government, finance, shipping, trade, transportation, and many small industries. Life in Corinth was often precarious; for outlaws, vigilantes, and terrorists, violence was the backup method for achieving their ends. Luke tells us in Acts 18 that Paul experienced, and feared, the threats in Corinth but was assured of God's protection. Finally, Paul discovered that many people were receptive to the gospel. Indeed, the Holy Spirit assured him that "there are many in this city who are my people" (Acts 18:10).

North America will soon look like a Corinthian continent. The U.S.A.'s population exceeds 280 million and is growing. The industrialization of the country, followed by revolutions in technology and transportation, has shifted the population well past 80 percent urban. The waves of immigration from Western Europe, Eastern Europe, Asia, and Latin America have transformed the nation into the most multicultural nation-state on earth. We have long been aware of the population mosaics in cities such as New York, Chicago, Los Angeles, and Miami; but most of the nation's cities have become much more multicultural than the cultural majority knows. For instance, the ESL staff of the Lexington, Kentucky, school board reports that its children speak at least forty-seven different languages in their homes. The peoples of the earth bring their languages, cultures, and religious worldviews with them. Across the

U.S.A., Muslim mosques have surfaced—from New York to Reno, from Nashville to El Paso.

We observe two other important parallels between ancient Corinth and the U.S.A. today. First, the country is even more vulnerable to multiple threats of conflict and violence; the country's legacy of pirates, outlaws, vigilantes, mobs, gangs, and the Mafia is now amplified by the encroachment of drug cartels, terrorist networks, and guns everywhere. The series of violent events such as the assassinations of the 1960s, the Unabomber, Columbine, Oklahoma City, Washington, D.C., and New York City's World Trade Center remind us of life's fragility.

Second, we observe an unprecedented harvest of open, receptive, searching people who are looking for life, often in all the wrong places. We observe the symptoms of this receptivity as people explore religious options from astrology to Zen, and self-help books, exotic new therapies, and drug-induced experiences. In the middle of this harvest, 80 percent of the nation's churches are stagnant or declining—which leads to our second major theme.

A Dysfunctional Church, with a Mission

Every casual student of the Bible knows that the ancient church in Corinth was, in the language of pop psychology, "dysfunctional." We find many examples of this church's dysfunction in Paul's two letters to the Corinthians; five examples illustrate their range of dysfunction. First, we discover in 1 Corinthians 1 that the church is split into ideological camps, representing exclusive attachments to Paul, or Apollos, or Cephas, or Christ. (We cannot assume the last group was the "good guys"; they may have been Gnostics, affirming Christ's divinity, but not his true humanity.) Second, some of the Corinthian Christians had imported non-Christian beliefs and moral practices into the life of the church, including several forms of sexual immorality.

Third, Paul refers to a church inflicted with "quarreling, jealousy, anger, selfishness, slander, gossip, conceit, and disorder" (2 Cor. 12:20). Fourth, the church lacked the unity that Christ wants for his church. Fifth, the church was not reaching its neighbors. A church in Corinth predated Paul's arrival. Priscilla and Aquila, a Jewish couple, had become Christians in Rome and then moved to Corinth when Claudius expelled Jews from Rome. When Paul arrived, he found a handful of Christians gathering with Priscilla and Aquila in their house church. So Paul found a church already there, but no Christian movement; the Christians were neither serving nor evangelizing the receptive peoples of Corinth.

How necessary is it to demonstrate parallel problems in the "mainline" (or "old line," or "sideline") denominations in North America today? Most denominations are split into ideological camps. Most denominations reflect, and parties within some denominations advocate, bewildering beliefs and moral practices. Groups within some denominations baptize their self-interest, conceit, and anger; they advance their causes through calculated quarreling, gossip, and slander. Professional ambition and jealousy are epidemic. The mainline denominations are so devoid of unity that the very name of my own denomination, The United Methodist Church, is an oxymoron—ranking with oxymorons such as "military intelligence," "business ethics," "civil engineer," "French deodorant," "British fashion," "Microsoft Works," and "faculty cooperation!"

Finally, like the church that Paul found in Corinth, the mainline churches of North America are not reaching their receptive neighbors. Although most churches are strategically placed amidst receptive populations, 80 percent of our churches are stagnant or declining. Of the 20 percent that are growing, 19 out of 20 are growing primarily by transfer growth and/or biological growth (or "Vatican roulette!"). Less than 1 percent of all the churches in North America grow substantially from conversion growth. Most churches do not reach out to their neighbors, nor do they expect, plan, budget, or pray to reach pre-Christian people.

So the Lord, as in first-century Corinth, is calling our dysfunctional churches to love, serve, and reach the peoples of an urban pluralistic society. (Notice, in contrast to the "church renewal" books that church leaders have read for many years, and in contrast to the "church health" books currently in vogue, churches are not called to become "renewed" or "healthy" first, and then to reach out. Pathological churches experience renewal and greater health as they abandon their narcissism, reach out, and experience new people who have just discovered grace entering their ranks.)

Paul's Prescription for Church Renewal

For decades, leaders who labor for church renewal have instinctively looked to Paul's two letters to Corinth for the keys to renewal. Five insights from these letters have been especially influential. First, scattered throughout his letters, Paul admonishes the Corinthian church to remain rooted in the gospel that they had received from him—a gospel of Jesus Christ crucified (1 Cor. 2:1) for our sins (1 Cor. 15:3), who was raised from death (1 Cor. 15:14) that people might know Jesus Christ as Lord (2 Cor. 4:5) and be reconciled to God (2 Cor. 5:18) and live the New Life: "He died for all, so that those who live might live no longer for themselves, but for him who died and was raised for them" (2 Cor. 5:15).

Second, renewal is rooted in a clear, shared identity; so, in 1 Corinthians 12, Paul teaches the Corinthian church that she is the Body of Christ, and in this Body we need one another as a human body needs each of its parts. Third,

Paul expresses the confidence in 1 Corinthians 11 that the Lord's presence in the Eucharist will bring believers together. Fourth, Paul teaches in 1 Corinthians 12 that the Holy Spirit "gifts" all believers for ministry; as people discover their gifts and get into ministry, the church is renewed. Fifth, in 1 Corinthians 13, Paul admonishes the believers to seek the higher spiritual gifts of faith, hope, and love and to "make love your aim."

All of those themes represent revealed Truth, and all are typically needed in a church's renewal. In organizations, including churches, no single intervention will fix a complex problem. Church renewal comes from many changes over time. The Corinthian truth, for most dysfunctional churches, however, goes even deeper than the need for multiple interventions. Unity comes from knowing who we are, knowing our main business, and pulling together to achieve it. Peter Drucker, the guru of the twentieth-century revolution in management, is fond of saying that there are only two questions that leaders of organizations need to be asking all the time: (1) What is our main business? (2) How is business?

The fifth chapter of 2 Corinthians is one of the most eloquent passages in Scripture, and a normative passage for understanding Christianity's identity and main business. Paul explains that, primarily, the Corinthian Christians are "ambassadors for Christ," that is, the authorized representatives of Christ to the peoples of Corinth and to peoples beyond. Our main business is "the ministry of reconciliation." God wants to reach other people through his Church. "God is making his appeal through us" (2 Cor. 5:20). It is our privilege to invite people to be reconciled to God and become followers of Jesus Christ.

Standing on Paul's shoulders, many advocates for Christianity's apostolic mission have approached his eloquence. Donald McGavran declared, "It is God's will that His Church grow, that His lost children be found." William

Temple claimed, "The true church is the only society in the world that exists for its nonmembers." Emil Brunner's identification of the connection between mission and faith substantially explains the struggle for faith in many churches: "The Church exists by mission as a fire exists by burning. Where there is no mission there is no church; and where there is neither church nor mission, there is no faith."

Lessons from the Snook, Texas, Foxhunting Club

One evening, perhaps fifteen years ago, Johnny Carson's *Tonight Show* featured two guitar-playing folksingers from Snook, Texas. Carson inquired, "What is notable about Snook, Texas? Does anything unusual ever happen in Snook?" The singers boasted that Snook has the only fox-hunting club in their region of Texas, and they reported that something unusual happened at the most recent fox-hunt. A new fellow had moved to town. He joined the club and brought his foxhound to the annual hunt. An official noticed that the new member's hound was female and recalled that all the other hounds were male. The club's constitution did not explicitly prohibit female hounds, so the new fellow's hound joined the eighty males for the hunt. Someone blew the bugle, and the dogs were off, baying the distinctive song of foxhounds on the hunt; the hunters, decked out in the distinctive red and black attire, rode on horseback behind them. The hounds outran the horses. The hunters lost sight of their dogs over a hill, but they kept riding. Eventually the hunters passed a farmer. They asked, "Did some foxhounds pass by here a few minutes ago?" "Yep," the farmer replied, "and the fox was running fifth!"

The casual viewer of that event might still have thought of it as a foxhunt. After all, all of the features of a foxhunt were in place: the bugle, the horses, the hunters, their attire, the guns, the hounds, the baying, and even a fox. But the farmer, a perceptive observer, discerned that what was now going on was no longer a foxhunt, but something very different. Although all of the components were still present, the agenda had changed completely. Subsequent commands and trumpeting from the hunters fell on 160 deaf ears.

This story of the foxhunt gone wrong serves as an (admittedly earthy) analogy of the condition of the mainline churches of the West. All of the components of the apostolic Christian movement that once won an empire are still in place: the gospel, the Scriptures, sacraments, sacred symbols, beliefs and ethics, worthy traditions, clergy and a gifted laity, a gathered worshiping community, hymns and prayers, and a hundred other recognizable features. Too often, however, underneath the veneer, the agenda has changed. The laity now obsess over their own needs and interests, maintaining the institution and perpetuating traditions as ends in themselves; whereas, too often, the clergy are protecting their jobs or advancing their careers or pursuing "politically correct" agendas or preparing for retirement.

They are no longer a Christian people on a mission, in any sense, that the early apostles would recognize. Indeed, they have redefined Christianity's main business to fit their changed agenda. Many Christians are like the eighty male hounds: Their revised agenda seems perfectly natural to them. Other Christians are like the fox: They prefer the current agenda to the original one. Occasionally, someone like the female foxhound will point out that the original mission has been abandoned, but they are barked or hounded into silence. Occasionally, even those people succumb to the tyranny of "group think," and it takes a complete outsider—such as the farmer—to point out the obvious, that the church has lost its identity and mission. All the while, the trumpet calls to mission from the Hound of Heaven are ignored.

This shift in the church's main business has occurred more at an unconscious than at a conscious level. Some church leaders, however, are confident that they have replaced Christianity's classical mission with something "better"; they network, build coalitions, get one another elected to leadership roles, and "work the system" for their ends. In the 1960s, these leaders hijacked the airplane of Christian mission that once departed for Jerusalem. They have redirected the plane toward their preferred destination—Philadelphia ("the city of brotherly love"). They observe, however, that the plane is no closer to Philadelphia than when they first hijacked it! Why? The hijackers have never understood that the Christian plane was originally bound for Philadelphia, *by way of Jerusalem*. Our colleagues have never understood that the only way Christianity's plane (indeed, humanity's plane) gets to Philadelphia is through Jerusalem.

We see all around us that Emil Brunner was right: Where there is no mission, there is no true church, and not much faith. Signs of hope, however, are surfacing all around us. Some of the leaders who once preferred the direct flight to Philadelphia have noticed that the plane is no closer to the Philly airport than when it was first redirected, say, forty years ago. Some leaders have "discovered" spirituality; and, as the Enlightenment fades with its promises unfulfilled, some leaders entertain the possibility that the Christian gospel might be true. Some leaders even hope it is true because their depressed spouse, their out-of-control teenager, or their addicted brother really does need to experience forgiveness, second birth, the love and grace of God in Christ, the Spirit's liberating power, and the fulfillment that comes from living as kingdom people. But once convinced that evangelization might be okay, desirable, or even Christianity's main business, they have no idea where to begin or how to go about it.

The Great Commission Manual

Paul's Corinthian correspondence becomes especially useful at this point. Throughout his two letters, Paul scatters so many insights about outreach ministry that the correspondence serves as a Great Commission manual. Let's feature eight of Paul's distinct insights.

(1) Paul informs the Corinthian church in 1 Corinthians 4 that Christians cannot, and must not, count on specialized "apostles" to reach all people. We know enough to affirm Paul's warning for several reasons. First, there are never enough apostles (or evangelists or missionaries or clergy) to go around. Second, cross-cultural ministry is always so difficult that the best strategy is for the cross-cultural apostle to reach a handful of converts and prepare them to minister and communicate the gospel, in ways natural to them, across their social networks to their cultural peers; the gospel spreads most when indigenous Christians multiply churches through indigenous evangelism. Third, Paul observed that the first-century apostles lacked credibility in much of the Mediterranean world; they were widely slandered, held in disrespect, and seen as fools.

Although we do not now understand all that was behind the public credibility problems of the first-century apostles, credibility problems afflict television evangelists and many other Christian advocates today. Indeed, pastors typically discover that they lose credibility with about half of the unchurched population the day they get ordained. For that reason, Herb Miller used to quip, "Evangelism is the only enterprise on earth where the 'amateurs' outperform the 'professionals' by two to one!" This is Paul's point. All of the People of God are "ambassadors for Christ"; outreach is a ministry of the laity. As American evangelists in the nineteenth century used to say, "Shepherds don't make new sheep; sheep make new sheep."

(2) *Credibility* is crucially important in the ministry of the laity. So Paul coaches the Corinthian church in 2 Corinthians 2 to understand that, as communicators of the gospel and "ambassadors for Christ," who we are and whose we are influences how we communicate and minister. "We are not peddlers of God's word," so we must not copy (say) the communication approach of a used-car salesman or a political candidate on the campaign trail or a celebrity in a television infomercial. Why? Because Christ's ambassadors reach out "as persons sent from God and standing in his presence." Our perceived authenticity is a crucial factor in whether people trust our message. Helmut Thielicke observed, in the secular Germany of the 1950s and 1960s, that "the credibility of the witnesser" is the greatest determiner in the believability of the message.[2] More recently, Ron Crandall's extensive questionnaire research discovered that converts responded, in part, because they could sense that their Christian friends were "connected to God."[3]

(3) Paul emphasizes in 1 Corinthians 12 and 14 that Christians are called, and gifted, by the Holy Spirit, to be in *ministry* with pre-Christian people; we do not merely preach or witness to people. We are entrusted with both "the message of reconciliation" *and* "the ministry of reconciliation" (2 Cor. 5:18-19). So the Holy Spirit gives believers "spiritual gifts" to be used in ministry within and beyond the Body of Christ. Indeed, the gift of tongues was given as "a sign . . . for unbelievers" (1 Cor. 14:22).

We know several reasons why we are called to ministry, and not merely to witness. First, the church in ministry establishes the credibility of its message. Second, because people are more than "souls with ears," we minister to the whole person, and often the whole family and society. Third, some of the gospel, and the lifestyle to which it calls us, is communicated and modeled nonverbally—by what the community of faith is doing and how it is living. Fourth, we meet our "higher needs" and experience purpose, meaning, and fulfillment much more through involvement in ministries than through witness alone (much less through church attendance alone). So we reach people, in part, by loving and serving them, by welcoming them into the fellowship of the faithful, and by praying with sick, struggling, possessed, and oppressed people. What we do in ministry, more specifically, depends on people's needs and the cultural context in which we minister. For instance, ministry to persons and families in the age of AIDS has required some contextual responses in ministry.

(4) In 1 Corinthians 9, Paul recommends that, in ministry and communication, we adapt to the language and culture of the people we are called to reach. Mission scholars identify this as the principle of "indigenous" Christianity, or "culturally relevant" ministry. At the surface level, an indigenous ministry strategy involves adapting to the style, the language, the aesthetics, and the music of the target population. (SLAM serves as a convenient acronym.) At a deeper level, indigenous ministry involves engaging the attitudes, beliefs, and values characteristic of the society, especially the core attitudes, beliefs, and values that provide the lens, or the "worldview," through which the society views the world.

Once, Paul had to battle for this principle because the culturally conservative Jerusalem church believed that Jewish customs were best for everyone who wanted to follow Jesus as Messiah. In Antioch, however, great numbers of Gentiles were becoming disciples—without submitting to circumcision, giving up pork, or becoming culturally kosher. The Jerusalem church, which served as the young movement's first headquarters, deployed Barnabas to intervene in the Antioch church. When Barnabas affirmed the church he observed in Antioch (in Acts 11) and declined to push them to adopt Jewish ways, this precipitated a crisis in the movement, and James—leader of the Jerusalem church—called a meeting. In this meeting, which the Christian tradition has named "the Jerusalem Council," Paul—with Simon Peter's timely support—persuaded the church to flex toward cultural relevance everywhere. This decision was momentous. It freed the Christian movement to adapt to every tongue, culture, and subculture on earth. That cultural flexibility enabled Christianity to become the world's most universal faith.

So in his first letter to the Corinthian church, Paul explains that there is only one gospel—"the message about the cross" (1 Cor. 1:18). For that reason, Paul explains in his early public ministry in Corinth, "I decided to know nothing among you except Jesus Christ and him crucified." Later, he explains that because the gospel is meant to be communicated meaningfully to all peoples of the earth, the effective communication of its meaning requires adapting to the indigenous cultural forms. So, to Jews, Paul communicates in Jewish ways; to the Gentile peoples, he communicates in ways natural to their respective culture: "I have become all things to all people, that I might by all means save some" (1 Cor. 9:22). Paul adapts to local cultures "for the sake of the gospel," and he admonishes all communicators of the gospel to do the same.

(5) Paul alludes to a *process* that is involved in communicating the gospel and reaching most people. He reminds the Corinthian church in 1 Corinthians 3:6, "I planted, Apollos watered, and God gave the increase" (KJV). My research with first-generation converts suggests that Paul's allusion is an understatement. With many people today, you have to clear away some rocks and other debris, and you have to plow and plant and water and fertilize and pull weeds; and often you plant a second or third time and replicate the fertilizing before God gives the increase.

Paul's allusion suggests five things that we know from

church growth research. First, as Paul and Apollos were both involved in the conversion of some of the Christians in Corinth, so evangelization is usually a "team game." Most converts report that several people served as their bridges and helped them find The Way; seldom do they name only one person.

Second, the process from a person's initial exposure to the gospel, to the point that he or she adopts it, takes time—weeks, months, or years, but usually months; knowledgeable Christians cooperate with this process.

Third (as chapter 7 of this book will elaborate), the leaders of Willow Creek Community Church maintain that the process involves a "chain" of experiences that leads to faith in God's good time; they suggest that each link in the chain matters, that our purpose in ministry at any given time is to provide one link in that chain, and that every link in the chain is important.

Fourth, my interview research with converts suggests that about thirty links are involved in the chain that leads to faith. (That is an estimated average, an approximation that varies significantly from one person to the next, depending, in part, on how "far back" in the process the witnessing community had to begin and the number and depth of the "issues" that the person brings to his or her encounter with the gospel.)

Fifth, my research has validated the insight in Charles G. Finney's *Lectures on Revivals of Religion*, that four sources (on which we elaborate in chapter 7) provide the links in the chain: (1) God's own sovereign action provides some of the links. (Indeed, God is orchestrating the whole chain to make it possible for the person to discover faith.) (2) Specific truths of the gospel, or specific texts of Scripture, provide some links. (Converts typically report one or several texts or truths that they could not get out of their minds.) (3) The compassion, ministry, witness, and character of people in the church provide some links.

(4) The convert is a very active agent in his or her own conversion. (Finney saw the convert doing more things and contributing more to the process than most evangelization theorists have seen; indeed, this was Finney's distinctive insight. The insight is essentially the same as the recovery movement's reminder to addicts to "work your program.")[4]

(6) Apostolic ministry intrinsically involves new church planting. This is nowhere stated in Paul's letters to Corinth, but everywhere presupposed. Scholars tell us that the church in each city associated with Paul was a federation of multiple "house churches"—small fellowships that met regularly in homes and came together for Sunday worship in some public place. My book *To Spread the Power: Church Growth in the Wesleyan Spirit* recalls this revealing experience:

> In 1979, I visited the ruins of ancient Corinth. Our tour guide paused at the site of Corinth's first house church. She explained that it did not long remain the city's only house church; soon, there were perhaps a half dozen others. Someone voiced the inevitable question: "Why so many house churches? Wouldn't one have been enough?" Our guide replied, "No, one house church would not have been enough." Ancient Corinth in the New Testament period was new; many people of many tongues lived here, and their various religions and philosophies were competitive. Christianity might not have survived here if the Christian movement had confined its strength to the number of people who could gather in one house church. As they started more house churches, they were able to grow—and not without them. "Besides," she said, "the second house church could reach some people the first could not, the third could reach still others, and so on."[5]

There were, more likely, a dozen or more house churches in Corinth when Paul first wrote to them. Within the apostolic period and since, serious Christian movements have

"multiplied units"—small groups, large groups, congregations, churches, ministries (and leaders)—*as* recruiting
units for new people.

(7) Near the end of his second letter, Paul challenged the
churches in Corinth to a wider mission that would reach
people, and peoples, beyond Corinth (2 Cor. 10). Paul probably had a regional mission strategy in mind. Once, he
spent two years with the Christian community in Ephesus
to prepare them for wider outreach in Asia Minor. The
strategy was effective; Asia Minor became the most
densely Christian province in the Roman Empire.

Likewise, Paul spent one and a half years in Corinth and
devoted the largest volume of his extant correspondence to
Corinth—doubtless preparing them to reach the peoples of
Achaia. So, he explains, "Our hope is that, as your faith
increases, our sphere of action among you may be greatly
enlarged, so that we may proclaim the good news in lands
beyond you" (2 Cor. 10:15-16). Achaia also became substantially Christian. The earliest local churches, in
Jerusalem and Antioch, were involved in the wider mission, and this pattern appears to have spread to the
churches Paul planted or influenced. Notice, they did not
just send money to support "the denomination's missionaries." The local churches sent and supported their own
missionaries to other peoples, and many members were
actively involved in the mission.[6]

(8) Most churches will experience this last mandate from
Paul's Corinthian letters to be the most challenging. Some
churches will find this mandate unthinkable, even revolt-
ing. However, the churches that risk obeying it will find it
revolutionary. Let me state it boldly: Jesus Christ calls his
churches to love and believe in, serve and reach out to, and
welcome and receive, those people and populations that
"establishment society" regards as hopeless, incorrigible,
unredeemable, "unlikely," or even "impossible," and to
deploy their converts in witness and ministry.

On this issue, Paul indulges in notorious specificity. He had observed that Corinthian society took a dim view of the worth or possibilities of any person who was "sexually immoral or greedy, or [was] an idolater, reviler, drunkard, or robber" (1 Cor. 5:11). In 1 Corinthians 6:9-10, Paul provides another suggestive list of "hopeless" people, which partly overlaps with the first: "Fornicators, idolaters, adulterers, male prostitutes, sodomites, thieves, the greedy, drunkards, revilers, robbers."

Most Christians are quite aware that Paul warns Christians not to associate with such people, not even to eat with them—a policy with which most "ghettoized" Christians are remarkably compliant. It is unfortunate that the one command we are so good at keeping is flagrantly misunderstood! Paul is telling the Corinthian Christians "not to associate" with any adulterer, thief, and so on, "who bears the name of brother or sister." Christians, he is saying, must dissociate from *professing Christians* who blatantly violate God's will and the moral norms of society.

Paul seems to be mandating this policy for two reasons. Dissociation is necessary, first, for the credibility of the church and its message; out-of-control Christians have always damaged the public credibility of Christianity. This is necessary, second, for the sake of the sinner among us. The principle is essentially the same as that behind a family's "intervention" with an addict who is out of control, self-destructing, and in denial. In the intervention, the family dramatizes this message: "From this moment on, you have no family and no support, and your most valued friendships will not be available to you, until you accept help and get into treatment and recovery." To encourage their repentance, we withdraw from Christians who continue in a profligate lifestyle until they repent.

Most important, Paul is declaring that we are in mission to lost people who need to be found, especially to the very people society regards as the most lost, irredeemable, and impossible. Paul was aware that we follow a Messiah who was rejected by the "good people" of his society because he was "the friend of sinners." Paul establishes his point with the Corinthians in a way that would have permitted remarkably little "wiggle room." After his list of fornicators, thieves, and so on, he reminds them: "This is what some of you used to be. But you were washed, you were sanctified, you were justified in the name of the Lord Jesus Christ and in the Spirit of our God" (1 Cor. 6:11).

This audacious dimension of Christianity's mission is essential because, in every society, there are people groups not at all like the society's "best people." These groups may or may not be poor, and they are not always "nice," are often "out of control," are frequently "looking for life in all the wrong places." The established society usually brands them as "losers" (or the cultural equivalent). But the good news is that Ted Turner is half right in his perceptive statement that "Christianity is a religion for losers." He missed the other half of the truth, however: Christianity represents and, at its best, mediates the only power in the cosmos that changes "losers" into "winners." Apostolic Christianity, at its best, has always known this and has insisted on maintaining this most "vile" part of its mission because reaching the "normal" people partly depends on reaching the "hopeless" people. Why? Because in the redemption of the most "irredeemable" people, the power of God to save is revealed to all who have the eyes to see!

When I have advocated this understanding of the Church's apostolic mission in field seminars, one challenge always surfaces. This is the most recent version: "I do *not* believe that all of the drunks, prostitutes, and daredevils would become Christians if we opened the doors and said 'Come in.' " I respond: "Neither do I, but Paul is assuring us of two things: First, *some* of them will become Christians; Paul directs us to 'become all things to all people' that we might 'by all means save *some*.' Second, the phrase 'by all means' involves believing in them and identifying with them and engaging in culturally relevant outreach and ministry not merely opening the doors. I may need to remind you, and myself, that not all of the 'good' or 'normal' people will become Christians either; but wherever we reach some of the 'bad' or 'abnormal' people, we observe more of the good or normal people responding. In both cases, we *do not* know in advance who will become disciples and who will not; so we are called to reach out to all people and peoples—that 'whosoever believes . . . may have eternal life.' "

So, when John Wesley was asked what made eighteenth-century Methodism different from the polite, proper, and powerless conventional religion of his land, he gave this simple explanation: In the Methodist movement,

> The drunkard commenced sober and temperate. The whoremonger abstained from adultery and fornication, the unjust from oppression and wrong. He that had been accustomed to curse and swear now swore no more. The sluggard began to work. The miser learned to deal his bread for the hungry and to cover the naked with a garment. Indeed the whole form of their life was changed.[7]

Standing on Wesley's shoulders, William Booth counseled the Salvation Army to "go straight for souls, and go for the worst." And Booth left the whole church this memorable battle cry:

> While women weep as they do now, I'll fight; while little children go hungry, as they do now, I'll fight; while men go to prison, in and out, in and out, as they do now, I'll fight; while there is a drunkard left, while there is a poor lost girl upon the streets, while there remains one dark soul without the light of God, I'll fight—I'll fight to the very end.

CHAPTER TWO

A Short History of "Apostolic Ministry"

T he first chapter, drawing from Paul's two letters to the Corinthian house churches, suggested a standard so essential to an "apostolic" perspective on ministry that if a church hasn't got it here, it hasn't got it. Jesus Christ calls his churches to love, believe in, serve, reach out to, welcome, and receive those people and populations that society's "establishment" regards as unlikely or even hopeless, and to deploy their converts in witness and ministry.

A church devoid of this redemptive vision may well provide good "chaplaincy services" to a gathered colony of conventional believers. Indeed, this characterizes the main business of at least a quarter million churches in the U.S.A. alone, and the apparent objective of most divinity schools' curriculums is to provide more "chaplains" for such churches. So, most pastors understand themselves not as "fishers of men" (and women), but as "keepers of the aquarium." Indeed, it has not even occurred to most of the pastors who claim to be ordained in "apostolic succession" that they are thereby called to succeed the ancient apostles in ministry to pre-Christian populations.

Since local churches lose 6 percent (or more) of their members each year to death, transfer, or reversion to the world, they have to reach that many new people to "stay even." Most churches, however, do not even engage in replacement outreach; so 80 percent of the churches in the U.S.A. are declining, or somewhat stagnant, in their membership strength. Most of the conventional churches that do reach out and invite, however, mainly respond to people who take the initiative to visit the church. *If* they reach beyond their visitors, they target people who are like their members, only younger; they assume that they cannot reach most of the other people in the community.

In working with many churches over several decades, I have heard (or inferred) a lengthy list of the kinds of people who, by definition or assumption, cannot be reached. So, for instance, unchurched teenagers and college students and saxophone players are "too wild" to become Christians. And, "retired people who have not become Christians by now never will." And, "newcomers need to get settled first before some church bothers them." And, "those people who have lived here for awhile and haven't joined a church by now never will." And, "those people from Mexico (or Korea or Romania or Samoa) don't even speak English! How could they become Christians?" The people who wash their clothes at the laundromat are not "nice" enough to become Christians. "If the people who live on the other side of the tracks did come to church, they wouldn't even know when to stand up and when to sit down." The rich people, the most successful people, and the Ph.D.s "look down their noses at us"; the jet set, the jocks, the bodybuilders, the fashionable people, the glamorous people, and the artsy people all intimidate us. Addicted people (and their families), prisoners and ex-prisoners (and their families), "bikers and their kind," eccentric people, people with a mental illness, and people with "bad breeding" need not apply. A tall-steeple Los Angeles pastor once claimed, if you do not reach movie stars "on the way up," no church can reach them later.

That list of allegedly unreachable people groups could be extended ad nauseam. In broad categories, there are two kinds of people who the typical traditional church never engages and invites: (1) those not "refined" enough to feel comfortable with us and (2) those whose lives are too out of control, or too different from ours, for us to feel comfortable with them. (That adds up to a lot of people in many communities, a majority of the unchurched people.) Many churches want to follow Jesus Christ and be fishers of men and women, but the only fish they really want to catch are the fish that have already been cleaned.

How Church People Misperceive Lost People

This incapacity for church leaders to lift up their eyes and see where the fields are white unto harvest (John 4:35) is rooted in (at least) six specific misperceptions:

1. Most church leaders vastly exaggerate the difference between "us" and "them"; but when we pay the price to understand them, we recognize our own feelings and needs in them and realize, "There but for the grace of God go I." And, as we understand them, we come to love them.

2. Most church leaders vastly exaggerate the degree to which the lifestyle of any non-Christian population will be a "temptation" to Christians who offer them ministry; but when we meet them in outreach, especially in supportive team outreach, our desire increases to be used by God to set them free.

3. Most church leaders vastly underestimate the numbers of non-Christians and the degree to which they will be receptive if we reach out to them appropriately and persistently enough for them to be assured that they matter to us and to God; we often discover they have been searching for Life all along, but in all the wrong places.

4. Most church leaders have forgotten that the prevenient grace of God goes before us and that Christ's Spirit is with them, preparing their hearts, before we join him; for that reason, in reaching out to the lost, hurting, or estranged neighbor, we meet Christ anew (Matt. 25:31).

5. Most church leaders have not discovered that reaching "unconventional" people is the catalyst to reaching unchurched "conventional" people. When the nurses, schoolteachers, and insurance agents rub shoulders with the former playboys, call girls, and addicts who are now free and living new lives, they are often moved, and they see something of the power of God to "rescue the perishing." The profoundly changed life is, by far, the most compelling of the "signs and wonders."

6. Most church leaders have never known how much good radical outreach does for the souls of those who reach out and for the whole church. Churches are renewed more from a steady stream of "impossible" people who have just discovered the grace of God than from any half dozen "renewal ministries" combined. Many people now come to church to be near

the miracles! So change must take place at the level of social perception before most churches will move from tradition to mission. They must see the peoples of the earth more like God sees them.

Jesus' Ministry with "Impossible" People

Many people will recognize that an apostolic perspective toward the earth's, and the community's, peoples is consistent with the ministry that Jesus of Nazareth practiced and modeled. My reading of the Gospels, however, contrasts with that of Christian leaders who talk most about "God's preferential option for the poor" and trumpet the call to identify with the marginalized, oppressed, and (especially) the poor people of the earth. While I respect that school of thought, I believe it represents an ideological reading of Scripture that misses some of "the wideness of God's mercy." The Messiah, according to Matthew's Gospel, for instance, commissions his movement to make disciples *panta ta ethne* (Matt. 28:19-20), that is, among the clans, tribes, castes, ethnic peoples, and other people groups of the earth. Demonstrably, Jesus did not confine his ministry to the poor and closely related groups. This is obvious to Thomas Cahill, an encyclopedic historian. In *Desire of the Everlasting Hills*, Cahill identifies Jesus' two audiences: "the powerless" and "the powerful."[1]

Jesus often reached the powerful, specifically when they saw the healing, deliverance, or transformation of the powerless. Sometimes, as in Matthew's Gospel, Jesus' redemptive deed engages both types concurrently. In Matthew 8, Jesus heals a centurion's paralyzed servant and commends the centurion for his faith. In Matthew 9, he raises from death the daughter of a synagogue leader. Jesus earned a reputation as "the friend of sinners," and he said, "I have come to call not the righteous but sinners" (Matt. 9:12).

(Not all "sinners" are poor, oppressed, or marginalized; in Matthew 19, for instance, he offers Life to a rich young ruler.) In Matthew 11, when John the Baptizer's agent asks Jesus if he is the promised Messiah, Jesus replies: "Go and tell John what you hear and see: the blind receive their sight, the lame walk, the lepers are cleansed, the deaf hear, the dead are raised, and the poor have good news brought to them" (vv. 4-5).

Luke is vividly aware that Jesus ministers to "unlikely" people, in part, to reach the others. So, Luke is especially attentive to the range of ways the nonblind and nondeaf respond to Jesus' ministry. When Jesus liberated "a man who had the spirit of an unclean demon" the onlookers in Capernaum were "all amazed" (Luke 4:33). In Luke 5:24, Jesus heals a paralytic in the presence of scribes and Pharisees, "so that [all] may know that the Son of Man has authority on earth to forgive sins." The people did not fully get it, however; Luke reports, "Amazement seized all of them, and they glorified God and were filled with awe, saying 'We have seen strange things today' " (v. 26). When a crowd observed Jesus raise a widow's son from death, Luke reports, "Fear seized all of them; and they glorified God, saying, 'A great prophet has risen among us!' and 'God has looked favorably on his people!' " (Luke 7:16).

The response to Jesus' ministry was sometimes negative. In Luke 6, when Jesus healed a man's withered hand on the Sabbath, the observing Pharisees "were filled with fury" (v. 11). In Luke 8, when Jesus liberated a possessed man by transferring the demons to a herd of swine, the people responded with fear; though the formerly possessed man was now "clothed and in his right mind," Luke reports, "All the people of the surrounding country of the Gerasenes asked Jesus to leave them" (vv. 34, 37). So, we can infer from Luke that Jesus' ministry to possessed, paralyzed, and dead people often moved other people toward faith; if his ministry, however, violated a custom or threatened an economic interest, the response was often negative.

Jesus' ministry to three populations—the lepers, tax collectors, and zealots—demonstrates the range, and social dynamics, of his outreach.

1. Jesus' cleansing of lepers (as in Luke 5 and 17) expresses the range of his outreach. When a person contracted the type of leprosy in which the skin ulcerates, and, in time, fingers and toes are lost, the disease was the least of the person's problems. Such lepers were pronounced "unclean," banished from society, and avoided, feared, loathed, and despised. Consequently, lepers experienced unspeakable isolation and a low sense of self-worth. The healing of any leper was widely acknowledged as a miracle of God. When Jesus deployed the Twelve on their initial mission, one of their five assignments was to "cleanse the lepers" (Matt. 10).

2. It is significant that one of those twelve disciples, Matthew, had once been ranked with a group that Jews loathed even more than lepers—tax collectors. If lepers were down-and-outers, tax collectors were up-and-outers. The hated tax collectors were Jews who had "sold out" to Rome and now collected taxes for the enemy. It was common knowledge that they overtaxed their own people and that they lined their pockets with the difference. So Jews regarded tax collectors as traitors and criminals, in the same class as murderers and robbers. Matthew was not poor; he was affluent and had coercive power over other people. He did experience, however, what it is like to be marginalized and outcast. Jesus was making a profound social statement by including Matthew as a prominent member of the Twelve. This transformed tax collector

later wrote the first of the four Gospels of our canonical New Testament.

3. Simon the Zealot stands as the exemplar of a third type of population that Jesus reached. The Zealots were the party within Judaism that most opposed the political control of their land and people by Rome. They engaged in periodic guerrilla warfare, terrorism, and assassinations. They targeted Romans for assassination, and also Jews who were thought to compromise with the Romans—such as tax collectors. Establishment Jews regarded the Zealots as wild, irresponsible, out-of-control fanatics. The men who fought to the death at Masada, after killing their own wives and children, were Zealots. By including a changed Zealot within the Twelve, Jesus is dramatizing the transformative power of his kingdom for all who have the eyes to see. By including within his Twelve both a Zealot and a tax collector, Jesus is demonstrating the kingdom's power to create and unite a new humanity.

We have featured, too briefly, Jesus' ministry to powerless, marginalized, and "hopeless" people, such as paralytics and lepers and blind, lame, deaf, and even dead people. We also featured Jesus' ministry to people of some place and power, such as tax collectors, Zealots, and a rich young ruler. We could expand the examples to include thieves and harlots, Samaritans and Gentiles, and others. Jesus' friendship and ministry with women departed from Jewish norms. In each case, the recognition, liberation, or life change of "impossible" people communicates the nearness of God's presence and power to many other people. Jesus was modeling a major strategic approach that his apostolic movement was to follow in many seasons of its history to the present time.

Mission of the Apostles to Impossible People and Peoples

Jesus Christ mandated the apostles and their churches to expand his outreach ministry to the peoples of the earth. The term "apostle," with its derivative terms, is rooted in the Greek verb *apostellein,* "to send out," and the noun *apostolos,* "sent out." In the Acts of the Apostles, Luke sees the original apostles and their churches as "sent out" to reach pre-Christian populations; all Christians are "sent." The Latin word for "send" is *mittere,* so the terms "apostle" and "missionary" have nearly identical meanings. Theologians usually stress, however, that the original "Apostles" (with a capital *A*) met two criteria: (1) They had experienced the risen Christ (2) who had commissioned them to reach an unreached people. Because of the first criterion, scholars such as Carl Braaten consider the New Testament Apostles as:

> unique, once-for-all, and unrepeatable in later generations. After the first generation there could be no successors to the apostles. . . . Just as there would never have to be another Messiah, another incarnation of the Son of God, another crucifixion for the salvation of the world, another resurrection of the crucified Christ, so also there would never have to be another set of apostles, another set of primary witnesses to the risen Lord.[2]

David Bartlett's *Ministry in the New Testament* is clear that, even in the history recorded in the New Testament, no one after the original Apostles had died was regarded as an Apostle. "What is lacking in the New Testament is any sense that the apostolic office itself is passed on from generation to generation." All Christians, however, were entrusted with the message, ministry, and mission of the Apostles.[3]

Four other points about the early Apostles are worth noting:

First, the New Testament reports more Apostles than the Twelve and Paul; we know only some of their names: James, Apollos, Andronicus, and Junia (a woman). Indeed, Peter's address at Pentecost provided the grounds for the emerging movement's deployment of women in unprecedented ways. He claims that God's promise through Joel, that God would pour out his Spirit on all flesh— and "your sons and your daughters shall prophesy"—was now being fulfilled (Acts 2:17).

Second, since the early Apostles were also the normative theologians of early Christianity, the tradition has regarded orthodox apostolic teachings as a sign of a church's apostolicity—sometimes, however, without regard to whether the church is seriously in mission!

Third, for three centuries, the movement substantially maintained Jesus' outreach to overlooked, hopeless, incorrigible, and impossible people. The emperor Julian observed in the fourth century, "There were members in the Christian churches whom no other religious society would tolerate within their bounds."[4] For decades, many writers perpetuated the notion that the early church's ranks were largely confined to the poorest and most marginalized people, but more recent scholarship seems to have destroyed that simplicity.[5] Julian was right; early Christianity conspicuously included people the society's establishment had no use for, including up-and-outers as well as down-and-outers.

Fourth, many writers have perpetuated the notion that the apostles and others spread the faith through "preaching." Robert Scudieri, for instance, reports, "Their primary strategy was itinerant preaching. This was the same strategy given to the Twelve Jesus commissioned in the tenth chapter of Matthew."[6] One problem with this "explanation" emerges when we recall that Jesus instructed the Twelve to "proclaim the good news" *and* to "cure the sick, raise the dead, cleanse the lepers, cast out demons"

(Matt. 10:7-8). Their job description was *not* confined to preaching!

The other problem is rooted in the assumption that preaching is the main way, if not the only way, we communicate the gospel. (That assumption is rooted in the deeper assumption that what ordained people do accounts for any effectiveness that the Christian movement experiences. I will suggest that the facts warrant a very contrasting premise: The faith is spread more by laity than by clergy, and they spread it through many ways of communicating and through many expressions of ministry, not by preaching or by verbal witness alone.) Preaching, as the term is casually used by many writers, is a nonreflective term that obscures much more than it reveals. For many able to attach a meaning to it, the term *preaching* refers to a priest or pastor delivering an expository sermon, from behind a pulpit, to a gathered congregation, in a church sanctuary. Since nothing like that took place until the fourth century, the term cannot inform us what Christianity's advocates were doing for the first three centuries.

The term *preaching* does not do justice to the many forms of oral communication reflected in even the early "Jewish phase" of the early mission—reflected in the first ten chapters of the Acts of the Apostles. Several examples should be sufficient. Acts 2 presents Peter, on the public occasion of the Jewish day of Pentecost and probably in the open air, delivering a speech, responding to a question, reasoning with the people, exhorting the people, and inviting the people to repent, accept forgiveness, and be baptized. In Acts 3, Peter tells the story of the sacred history that begins with the promise to Abraham and is fulfilled in the life and death of the Messiah whom God raised. In Acts 4, Peter uses the questions confronting him in a court of law to explain the new gospel. In Acts 5, the apostles begin teaching the good news both in the temple courtyard and from house to house, presumably developing different themes and employing different approaches in the large temple courtyard setting than those for the small Christian house churches. Stephen uses a legal setting, in Acts 7, to offer a complete version of "The Story"; his prayer, "Lord, do not hold this sin against them," overheard as a crowd stoned him, had, undoubtedly, great communicative impact. In Acts 8, Peter and John engage in the ministry of conversation with Simon the Magician, and Philip converses with the Ethiopian eunuch, both conversations in response to requests or questions. Acts 10 records Peter's conversation with Cornelius. So, Acts 1–10 records oral communication—such as public address, storytelling, response to questions, teaching in large settings, instruction in more intimate settings, and two-way conversations—in a range of settings. Luke records *no* preaching in the (now) usual sense of expository pulpit preaching in a church.

Furthermore, the usual "explanation" that the gospel spread in Christianity's early history through preaching ignores the ways in which the apostles and their people communicated the gospel's meaning nonverbally, through other ministries, through worship, and through the lives of Christian people. Even in the Jewish phase of the early mission, the communication of Christian meaning also took place nonverbally. Since the first baptism recorded in Acts 2, that sacrament and the Lord's Supper have been experienced as "means of grace" and the "visible Word" of God. The ministries of healing, exorcism, and "signs and wonders" (Acts 5) communicated volumes, as did the new lifestyles of the early Christians—loving one another, holding their possessions in common, sharing with anyone in need (Acts 2), and welcoming strangers and seekers. Acts 9 features the life of Dorcas. Luke records nothing she ever said. "She was," Luke reports, "devoted to good works and acts of charity" (Acts 9:36). The number of people mourning her death presumably includes her converts. There is evidence that the early Christians prayed for people and prayed with people and "gossiped the gospel" and invited seekers into the fellowship of their house churches and to the large Sunday worship assemblies. Undoubtedly, many seekers found the Christian community's joyful expectation of the promised kingdom to be contagious.

Acts 1–10 records ministries that communicated through word and deed in combination (though the more usual sequence is deed, then word). In Acts 3:2, Peter engages "a man lame from birth" who is asking for alms. Peter says, "I have no silver or gold, but what I have I give you; in the name of Jesus Christ of Nazareth, stand up and walk" (v. 6). Peter took his hand, helped him get up, and the man walked. The onlookers, Luke reports, "were filled with wonder and amazement" (v. 10). In Acts 8, Philip ministered in "a city of Samaria" to lame, paralyzed, and possessed people, after which his remarks had the townspeople's full attention! In Acts 9, Peter spoke and served as the Holy Spirit's agent in healing a paralyzed man, and the man got up from his bed for the first time in eight years. Luke reports, "All the residents of Lydda and Sharon saw him and turned to the Lord" (v. 35). Throughout much of Acts, as people with dire afflictions are healed or delivered, and as "unlikely" people—such as Simon the Magician, the Ethiopian eunuch, Saul of Tarsus, and Cornelius ("a centurion of the Italian cohort")—become disciples, public interest in the gospel became more infectious.[7]

Luke's focus in the Acts of the Apostles is regrettably selective. The only two "stars" of the church's early expansion drama in Luke's account are Peter and Paul, with people such as Stephen, Philip, Barnabas, Silas, Apollos, and even John in supportive or cameo roles; Andrew and Thomas receive no significant mention. Furthermore, after Luke shows how the gospel spreads from Jews, to Samaritans, to Gentiles, he reports its spread much more in terms of cities, islands, or regions—such as Cyprus,

Antioch of Pisidia, Iconium, Lystra, Derbe, Macedonia, Thessalonica, Beroea, Athens, Corinth, Ephesus, Troas, Miletus, Malta, and Rome. He doesn't tell us much about the other peoples whom the early Christian movement reached.

Fortunately, later traditions about the apostles take up more or less where Acts of the Apostles ends. Writings such as Acts of Andrew, Acts of John, Acts of Paul, Acts of Peter, Acts of Thomas, Acts of Philip, Acts of Barnabas, and even "The Apostolic History of Pseudo-Abdias" tell us much more about where the apostles journeyed, the people groups they evangelized, and the ways they engaged in ministry.

Unfortunately, like many ancient writings, these writings embellish the character, the experiences, and the achievements of the original apostles beyond what even twenty-first-century standards of journalism permit! For instance, the many legends that circulated by the second century had several apostles proclaiming the gospel in more languages and planting the church among more peoples, in more places, often concurrently, than would have been possible. Various traditions connect Matthew with Ethiopia, Persia, Parthia, and Macedonia. Various legends place Philip in Lydia, Parthia, Gaul, and, most credibly, Asia. Today, Andrew is regarded as the patron saint of four countries—Russia, Greece, Romania, and Scotland.[8]

Some of the stories and descriptions go beyond mere legend. In Acts of Philip, for instance, we are told that the apostle advocated the Christian faith to an assembly of three hundred philosophers in Athens. The philosophers sent to Jerusalem for the Jewish high priest, Ananias, to refute Philip. Ananias arrived with an entourage of five hundred men bent on killing Philip, but Philip struck all five hundred men blind and ordered the earth to swallow Ananias. The men in Ananias's (now blind) battalion converted and were baptized along with many Athenians, and Philip stayed long enough to found the church there.

Again, the Apostolic History of Abdias leaves us this remarkable description of Bartholomew:

> He has black, curly hair, white skin, large eyes, straight nose, his hair covers his ears, his beard long and grizzled, middle height. He wears a white robe with a purple stripe, and a white cloak with four purple gems at the corners. For twenty-six years he has worn these, and they never grow old. His shoes have lasted twenty-six years. He prays a hundred times a day and a hundred times a night. His voice is like a trumpet; angels wait upon him; he is always cheerful, and knows all languages.

This description illustrates how, in many of the accounts in this legendary material, an educated reader can discern the probable from the improbable.

Although the traditions may put some of the Apostles in too many places concurrently, they are very clear about the kinds of "impossible" peoples the early apostles often engaged. The Jews perceived Rome to be particularly cruel and degenerate; the tradition believes that Peter cared enough and dared enough to take the faith there. The Scythians were widely regarded as crude animal-like "barbarians"; the tradition strongly reports that Andrew reached them and planted a Scythian church. The tradition tells us that Matthew reached the land of the Anthropophagi—cannibals. Matthew ministered, healed sick people, exorcised demons, and taught the gospel among them. The king became jealous of Matthew's power and had him executed; but then the king repented and became a priest, and many of his people turned to the Christian faith. A number of the apostolic legends report apostles reaching such peoples as barbarians and cannibals.

Several of the "Apocryphal Acts" and other second-century

writings feature apostles in ministry with persons thought unsalvageable. While in Ephesus, John saw great promise in a young man. At John's recommendation, the bishop took the young man into his home, baptized him, and taught him. The young man, however, was influenced by evil peers; he became a robber and, in time, chief of a robber band. When John returned to Ephesus some years later, he was distraught by the report of the young man's choices. Drawing from Clement of Alexandria, William Barclay completes the story:

> John called for a horse and a guide and rode straight from the church to find the youth. When he came near to the headquarters of the robber band he was captured by the robber's sentries. He made no effort to escape. "It was for this very purpose that I came," he said. "Take me to your leader." So he was brought to the leader, who was waiting fully armed, but when he recognized John, he was smitten with shame and turned and fled from his presence. Forgetting his old age, John pursued him. "Why do you flee from me, my child," he said, "from your own father, from me a poor, old, unarmed man? Have pity upon me, and do not fear. You have still hope of life. I myself will give account to Christ for you. If need be, I will willingly undergo your penalty of death, as the Lord did for us. I will give my own life in payment for yours. Stand! Believe! Christ has sent me!" On hearing this the youth threw away his weapons and fell to trembling and to tears. With bitter contrition he repented, and John assured him that he had found pardon with his Savior for him. He prayed with him; he brought him back to the church; he never ceased to keep his grip upon him; and in the end the young man was so changed by Christ that he became the bishop of the congregation.[9]

The Acts of Andrew features the apostle in a range of ministries in his field of mission. The text makes *no* mention of Andrew doing any preaching, though he does address the townspeople before his execution. Andrew engages people in the ministry of conversation, he responds to questions, he teaches the gospel and its ethic to seekers and new believers, he teaches and interprets the Lord's Prayer, and he counsels people in their struggles and moral choices. His most visible public ministry is with prisoners—who were believed to be hopeless—and, in his healing ministry, he targeted people with "ailments . . . which many considered beyond help"; and he uses the healing of a beloved servant to reach Stratocles, a man of some local power.

In his conversation with Stratocles, a troubled man, Andrew proposes to "bring out into the open the person now latent within you." "Already," Andrew observes, "your new self speaks to me. . . . He is ashamed of his former religion [and life]. . . . He now knows that it was hollow, . . . destitute, worthless, . . . that it promises nothing essential. . . . Is that not so? Does the person inside you say these things, Stratocles?" Stratocles felt so understood that he knew Andrew must be "a messenger of the living God." The two men become close, spending many days and nights together, with Andrew responding to Stratocles' many questions. Andrew included the emerging colony of believers in this ministry; as they heard Stratocles' questions, and Andrew's answers, they saw the power of the ministry of conversation, and they understood how the group could support Stratocles in his quest. In time, the people could see changes in Stratocles' life and manner and that he "possessed a steady soul and a firm and unalterable faith in the Lord."

The Church's (Reluctant) Mission to Rural Peoples

When Julian observed "members in the Christian churches whom no other religious society would tolerate within their bounds," he was probably unaware that the church, by the fourth century, had actually lost much of the earlier "catholic" view that believed Christianity was for all humanity and that hopeless people are often far more reachable than established society perceived. Following the conversion of Constantine, when Christianity transitioned from persecuted faith to the Roman Empire's preferred faith, the church became more "establishment." State funding shifted from the pagan temples to the church, congregations moved from humble structures to lovely buildings, sons of aristocrats now entered the priesthood, and the church took on a more "establishment" view of the human race. By, or before, the fourth or fifth century, this change negatively affected Christianity's mission in regard to two major categories of people.

First, early Christianity was an *urban* religious movement. The faith's people transported the gospel as they traveled the Roman roads and the sea-lanes to the Roman Empire's cities. In time, the church widely assumed that the more backward rural peasant populations of the Roman Empire were not appropriate candidates for Christianization. Richard Fletcher summarizes the urban cultural attitudes that undermined Christianity's outreach to country people for two centuries:

> Civilization and culture were to be found exclusively in cities. . . . Most townspeople, most of the time, looked upon the rural peasantry with mingled disgust, fear and contempt. They were dirty and smelly, unkempt, inarticulate, uncouth, misshapen by toil, living in conditions of unbelievable squalor, as brutish as the beasts they tended. . . . The peasantry of the countryside were beyond the pale, a tribe apart, outsiders. . . . The countryside simply did not exist as a zone for missionary enterprise. After all, there was nothing in the New Testament about spreading the Word to the beasts of the field.[10]

We know of no serious mission to rural peoples until the pioneering work of Saint Martin of Tours in Gaul from A.D. 371 to 397.[11] Saint Martin was prepared for this unprecedented challenge. He contrasted with the typical "well heeled, well connected, well read, well groomed" bishops of the fourth century.[12] He was a former soldier, modestly educated, earthy, and unconventional; he dressed like a peasant and rode a donkey rather than a horse befitting a bishop. He took a confrontational slash-and-burn approach to the people's primal religion, but, wherever he destroyed a pagan temple, he built a church. Martin and his successors built at least two monastic communities, from which they built a web of churches in the region's rural settlements. Martin's monastic community at Tours is missiologically significant because it was the first to prepare people for mission, it was the first mission to rural peoples, and because the young Patrick later spent time there, reflecting his way into an approach that would contrast with Martin's. Martin's mission to rural peoples is significant because he demonstrated that a population widely assumed to be unredeemable might, indeed, be reached if approached right. In time, the Church of Rome caught on and the Empire's rural populations became substantially Christian.

The Church's (Reluctant) Mission to "Barbarian" Peoples

The church's long-held assumption that rural people were unreachable, however, was but the first chapter in a lengthy volume. For over eighteen hundred years, the church's mission has been undermined more by some version of the assumption that such and such a population is "impossible" to Christianize, than by any other single cause. Often, the church's resistance to reaching out has far exceeded any resistance in the target population to being reached! The biggest case, the most enduring, that has taken many forms for many centuries is the case of the "barbarians."

In the same period that church leaders assumed rural peoples within the Roman Empire were hopelessly lost and incapable of becoming real Christians, they assumed this, even more, of the known "barbarian" peoples of Europe—the Vandals, the Goths, the Visigoths, the Franks and Frisians, the Lombards, Celtic peoples, Slavic peoples, Scandinavian peoples, and so on. Culturally, Roman people, including church leaders, considered any people group to be barbarian if it did not read and write; if it did not speak, read, and write Latin; and if they had not adopted Roman customs. If they were not culturally Roman, they were not "civilized"; and if they were not "civilized," it was doubtful they could become "Christianized."[13] This assumption immobilized the wider mission that, we now know, was clearly possible. Consequently, E. A. Thompson tells us, "Throughout the whole period of the Roman Empire not a single example is known of a man who was appointed bishop with the specific task of going beyond the frontier to a wholly pagan region in order to convert the barbarians living there."[14]

Patrick set in motion the movement that changed all of that. Patrick grew up in a Latin-speaking clan within a Briton tribe in (what is now) northwest England. At sixteen, Patrick was abducted by pirates and sold into slavery in Ireland, where he spent six years herding cattle before his escape. In those six years of slavery, Patrick missed his "high school" Latin education, but he came to Christian faith and came to love his captors, learn their tongue and customs, and reflect upon ways they might be reached. About twenty-five years after his escape, in A.D. 432, he returned with an apostolic band to commence Christianity's mission to Ireland's Celtic tribes. By the time of the death of the apostolic bishop to the Irish in A.D. 460, perhaps 40 of Ireland's 150 tribes had become substantially Christian; two generations later, all of Ireland was reached.

In time, this Celtic Christian movement deployed Columba, Aidan, and Columbanus, each with an apostolic band, to reach the Picts of Scotland, the Anglo-Saxon peoples that now populated England, and the barbarian peoples of Europe, respectively. In each mission, they built the monastic communities, from which they planted the churches, and from which they reached "barbarian" peoples. The Roman branch of the church was finally assaulted by "a blinding flash of the obvious" for a second time and deployed Boniface and others in the wider mission that, in time, reached Europe for a second time.[15]

So, Martin's movement in Gaul demonstrated that rural peoples could be reached after all, and the movement Patrick launched demonstrated that barbarian peoples could be reached after all. To the credit of "headquarters," they changed their minds in the face of compelling evidence. But church leaders—local, regional, national, or global—have virtually never experienced the wider paradigm shift that has them initially assuming that a "different" people probably *can* be reached. Our leaders usually assume that they cannot be reached or, if reached, cannot become real Christians "like us." As one example among many, in 1796 the General Assembly of the Church of Scotland adopted the following statement: "To spread abroad among barbarians and heathen natives the knowledge of the Gospel seems to be highly preposterous, in so far as it anticipates, nay even reverses, the order of Nature."[16]

Three Cases—Two Global, One Local

It usually takes a leader, such as Martin or Patrick, who is outside of the "Christian establishment," and who isn't

61

educated enough in establishment thinking to know what is "impossible," to more accurately perceive a frontier and the ways to penetrate it. Three cases should illustrate this sufficiently.

In eighteenth-century England, the closure of the "common lands" and the Industrial Revolution's creation of jobs combined to "push" people out of the countryside and to "pull" people into the cities by the hundreds of thousands. It seems that virtually nowhere did the city churches of the established Church of England see this urban population influx as an opportunity. The new urbanites lacked the level of literacy, the couth, the attire, the refinement, the "class," the obvious means to rent pews, and the "church etiquette" that made them "fit" to be invited to church. The myth is widespread that the Church of England had "the common people" of England's cities but lost them. Actually, it never had them, never invited them, and never seemed to want them.

Although John Wesley was a boy in Epworth, he had learned some things from his mother, Susanna, about reaching common people. Later, as a student at Oxford, he engaged in ministry with prisoners, prostitutes, and destitute people. When George Whitefield began reaching miners and their families near Bristol in 1739, Wesley began to perceive that an evangelical movement might be possible among the very populations that the established church had given up on. Wesley, with a band of people, itinerated the cities and towns of England, engaging in ministry, conversation, and open-air advocacy, and starting Methodist "classes" and "societies" with converts and awakened seekers.

Wesley's credibility, and legend, grew from his ministry with mobs! In Wednesbury, England, for instance, a thrown brick grazed his shoulder on one occasion; on another occasion, a stone struck him between the eyes; and other times, he was struck with fists and sticks. When he returned to the town in October of 1743, a mob approached the house where he stayed, calling, "Bring out the minister; we will have the minister." In his journal, Wesley reports what happened next:

> I desired one to take their captain by the hand, and bring him into the house. After a few sentences interchanged between us, the lion was become a lamb. I desired him to go and bring one or two more of the most angry of his companions. He brought in two, who were ready to swallow the ground with rage; but in two minutes they were as calm as he. I then bade them make way, that I might go out among the people. As soon as I was in the midst of them, I called for a chair; and, standing up, asked, "What do any of you want with me?" Some said, "We want you to go with us to the Justice." I replied, "That I will, with all my heart."[17]

Wesley did go with the people to explain their grievance to the Justice. Often, he addressed mobs, but he engaged their leaders in conversation, one-on-one, and found ways to show that he, and God, were on their side. Wesley reports in this journal entry that several of the "captains of the rabble" during his earlier engagements in Wednesbury later became men whose "hearts were turned."

By Wesley's death in 1791, Methodism in England was over seventy thousand strong and had spread to Scotland, Ireland, America, and the Caribbean, everywhere targeting the peoples unreached, ignored, and often regarded as impossible by the churches that preceded Methodism's arrival. By reaching "common people" who experienced profound life change, Methodism also reached and involved people of means and influence; Lady Huntingdon was the most notable example. Wesley reflected upon this dynamic in his journal: "I preached at Haddington, in Provost D's yard, to a very elegant congregation. But I expect little good will be done here, for we begin at the wrong end: *religion must not go from the greatest to the least, or the power would appear to be of men.*"[18]

The twentieth-century pentecostal movement serves as a recent large-scale case of this apostolic dynamic. Indeed, no fiction writer or Hollywood producer could imagine a more unlikely person than William Joseph Seymour, or a more unlikely place than a renovated warehouse on Azusa Street in a poor section of Los Angeles, to begin a movement that would reach more unlikely people than Pentecostalism has reached in less than a century. Harvey Cox reports:

> After two decades of preliminary stirrings, what is now called the "Pentecostal movement" burst forth . . . amid unpromising circumstances in a run-down section of Los Angeles. Led by an African-American preacher with no theological education, its first adherents were poor domestic servants, janitors, and day workers—black and white—who had the audacity to claim that a new Pentecost was happening, the New Jerusalem was coming soon, and that they were its designated heralds and grateful first fruits.[19]

Every interpreter of Pentecostalism[20] is impressed by the movement's engagement and inclusion of many poor, uneducated, marginalized, disinherited, left-behind, and even outcast "losers" at the bottom of society's social ladder, and by the movement's power to convince them that they need to change and that the Spirit can empower their change and will "gift" them for ministry and make their lives significant. The movement, on every continent, makes "losers" into "winners." Pentecostalism seems more able to achieve interracial fellowships, and to recognize and empower women for ministry, than any other branch of Christianity. In addition to reaching "the masses," many people of "the classes" are attracted to Pentecostalism's hope, life, changed lives, and more inclusive humanity. The movement has often observed that cynics "came to scorn and stayed to pray."

The Pentecostal movement's spread has been unprecedented in the history of Christianity. In the first six months of the Asuza Street Revival, thirty-eight people came to observe, and then they fanned out with the message to every continent. The movement reaches both marginal people from the traditional churches and people who have never before been Christian disciples. The movement now reaches more than 20 million people each year; its ranks are now reported to exceed 400 million, approaching 500 million.

Bill Borden was the heir of the Borden Dairy empire. He discovered faith in Christ at Moody Church in Chicago, and, in 1909, he enrolled as an undergraduate student at Yale. When Samuel Zwemer, the champion of Christian mission to Muslim peoples, spoke at Yale, Borden knew God was calling him to mission. After graduation, Borden renounced his inheritance, sailed to Egypt, and prepared for a mission assignment by studying Arabic. He contracted spinal meningitis, however, and died within weeks. He left this simple message: "No reserve, no retreat, no regrets."[21] His story inspired thousands of Christians into missionary vocations.

My colleague who teaches courses in "spiritual formation" at Asbury, Reg Johnson, recently shared a sequel to the story of Bill Borden, a story of one of many people who committed to mission in the wake of Borden's death. Lucy Peet was a Palmolive Peet heiress in Chicago. She was to have married Bill Borden. Following a period of grief and self-discovery, she became a Baptist home missionary and settled, in 1915, in Lynn, North Carolina—a mountain village of about a thousand people, with no church. She found a handful of believers; they began meeting together for prayer and Scripture study. She asked her people to list the persons in Lynn who'd be hardest to reach. One name was on every list—Jess Arledge. Arledge, they said, was not a bad man, but he was notoriously unreliable; alcohol had such a powerful grip on him that he squandered his paychecks on liquor. He existed with his wife, Carrie, and two children, a boy and a girl, in a small cabin with a dirt floor. The children often had no shoes. People took them food and clothing at Christmas.

The group befriended Jess Arledge and prayed for him; in time, they included him in their fellowship. Within six months, he was profoundly converted. He was delivered from the tyranny of alcohol, and the community now knew a sweet, kind, engaging man. He lived for another three years, before he died from tuberculosis. Many people were moved as they observed the Jess Arledge miracle unfold in their community, and Arledge joined the group, reaching almost one hundred townspeople. The Lynn Baptist Church was officially established. Jess Arledge emerged as a stalwart leader. Many charter members were baptized as new Christians.

Following Jess Arledge's death and his celebrative funeral at the church, Jess Arledge's widow, Carrie, moved to Durham to find employment. Lynn Baptist Church continued to grow. Jess and Carrie's son lived with relatives, and their daughter lived with Lucy Peet for almost two years, until Carrie could support them. The daughter, Hazel, grew up to be a strong Christian woman; and one day, she married Clarence Johnson. One of her children is my colleague Reg. Now, as Paul Harvey says, you know the rest of the story.

Reg Johnson's story is unique only in its specifics. Virtually every person who was raised a Christian could experience that privilege only because some missionary Christians once believed in what an ancestor could become by the grace of God. Every church is entrusted with the opportunity to birth Christward movements in many families for many generations.

CHAPTER THREE

Apostolic Ministry Through "Cultural Relevance"

W e have discussed several ideas that are crucial to Western Christianity's future viability: As in ancient Corinth, "dysfunctional churches" are called to serve and reach the people and peoples of our urban multicultural society. This mission involves planting new churches, reaching people of other lands and cultures, and especially reaching "way out" to "hopeless" or otherwise "unlikely" people and peoples.

We saw in chapter 2 that this understanding of the Great Commission Project is rooted in the ministries of Jesus and the early apostles and their churches. Chapter 4 will show that this apostolic vision of Christianity's main business has often been obscured by a clergy-centered, maintenance-oriented approach to "doing church," but God has often raised up leaders, churches, and movements—such as the Celtic, Wesleyan, and Pentecostal movements—to recover the essential mission of the whole Church.

This chapter expands on the theme from 1 Corinthians that we are called to emulate Paul in being "all things to all people"; we are called to adapt to the cultures of the peoples we serve and reach, that we might "by all means save some" (1 Cor. 9:12-23).

The Unconscious Pathology of Old East Side Church

Christianity's mission to pre-Christian populations, transparently, is not the agenda of traditional Old East Side Church on the corner of Maple Street and Jefferson Avenue. Like the foxhunt in Snook, Texas, Old East Side Church is engaged in frenetic activity, but the church is distracted from its original main business, and has been for decades. I have consulted with many churches like Old East Side and have studied many more. I ask "simple questions," such as, "When this church gets to where it's going, where will it be?" "What is this church's main business?" Often, the leaders of Old East Side and other churches are mute in response to such elementary questions. Or, each leader in the church voices his or her own response; the church has no consensus direction. The nearest to a consensus typically relates to perpetuating the tradition, maintaining the institution, or caring for "our people."

I have especially noticed that Old East Side Church (like the 300,000 similar churches across the U.S.A.) does not produce, in appreciable numbers, the kind of laity who engage in ministry, witness, and invitation to people outside the church's membership. The church's surrounding ministry area is filled with more pre-Christian people than ever, people who are more receptive than ever. Old East Side, however, is not gathering the harvest, has no plans to gather the harvest, and may not even perceive the harvest. To put it another way, most churches are placed in a pond stocked with more hungry fish than ever before; over half of those churches are not catching enough fish to replace the ones they lose to death, transfer, or reversion to the world.

Six Indicators That Old East Side Is in "Deep Weeds"

I have especially noticed six features of churches like Old East Side Church:

1. Old East Side's people do not reach out. They almost never invite someone with no Christian background or who isn't already on the church's fringe. I recall, for example, the results of a research project done about twenty years ago, which reported that it takes the average Episcopalian twenty-eight years to make a new Christian from the world.[1]
2. Old East Side Church cannot reach and then retain the growing number of "secular people" who have no prior Christian background or memory.[2] They do reach such persons, occasionally, as when a secular person marries a church member; but the odds of that person being totally inactive twelve months later are much higher than those for the people who joined by transfer the same Sunday.
3. Old East Side Church has substantially lost the vision it once had for mission, local and global. Once, the church was involved in world mission, gave almost half its budget to mission, and inspired several members to volunteer for mission vocations. That era, however, is no longer a living memory; like most of the

other "mainline" churches across the U.S.A., Old East Side's current members now cannot recall the time their church, or denomination, had a serious world mission. Sociologist Rodney Stark reports that, in 1880, the U.S.A.'s mainline churches provided over 18 out of every 20 Americans serving as foreign missionaries. By 1935, they provided less than 10 out of every 20. "In 1996, they sent out fewer than 1 out of 20."[3]

4. Old East Side Church cannot retain a bare majority of its own young people into adult discipleship. This is the dirty little secret of Protestant Christianity in the U.S.A. With its teenagers, Old East Side practices a form of "insanity"—defined by the Recovery Community as "doing the same thing over and over, each time expecting a different result."

5. Old East Side Church still "does church" much like it did in the 1950s. Consequently, the church has changed so little in the last half century, a period during which the people and the culture of the ministry area have changed so much, that Old East Side can no longer graft "a good evangelism program" on to the church and expect anything to happen for more than a season. Why?

6. The evangelism program will experience a short life because Old East Side Church is "stuck" in a way of "doing church" that is a "spent force." The church functions as though its leaders expect next year will be 1957. So the church will be strategically positioned *if* 1957 ever rolls back around again! If it does not, however, Old East Side's trajectory guarantees that outsiders will one day experience them as the Amish people of the mid–twenty-first century—people who perpetuated an old way of doing church and living as Christians into a vastly changed culture.

Old East Side's Losing Game Plan

I have observed and interviewed in hundreds of churches more or less like Old East Side Church. To their credit, they seldom want their people to be mere nominal Christians; they usually *want* their people to live as Christians in their homes and communities and to engage in ministry, witness, and invitation. They often hope for it, pray for it, and even exhort their people to be more committed to a life of serious discipleship. But it seldom happens. Why?

Although the people are not blameless, we can observe a larger cause in the way Old East Side "does church." The church's approach to forming disciples no longer produces the kind of Christians the church says it wants. Dietrich Bonhoeffer once observed, "The rusty swords of the old world are powerless to combat the evils of today and tomorrow." Likewise the traditional model of doing church is increasingly powerless to produce the kind of Christians who will reach the people in the community and who want what Christianity has to offer (but isn't offering).

Traditional American "Churchianity" draws from two deep roots: (1) the English, Scottish, Swedish, German, or other European culture from which the denomination crossed the Atlantic in, say, the eighteenth century, and (2) the 1950s, when the U.S.A.'s mainline denominations last flourished. The typical traditional church thus perpetuates a "blended" way of doing church; most of the features in the music, liturgy, government, pastor's job description, and so on, reflect, say, the Scottish Christianity that thrived in the 1700s and the American Christianity that thrived in the 1950s.

That traditional approach is ineffective today because the surrounding community's culture (or cultures) is not where it was in the 1950s, and the surrounding culture is even less like the European culture from which the denomination came in, say, the 1700s. (Indeed, Europe's cultures have changed, too; so, for instance, the traditional Presbyterian model for doing church inherited from the Church of Scotland is no more reproductive, today, in Scotland than in the U.S.A.)

What is that traditional approach? What do traditional churches count on to build people? As I have observed and interviewed in traditional churches for years, I have inferred a "five-point game plan" that Old East Side seems to be implementing year after year.

What is that game plan? We can state it cogently: Old East Side Church wants people to (1) attend church, (2) attend Sunday school, (3) attend other church programs, (4) have a daily devotional, and (5) have regular pastoral care from an ordained pastor or priest. One can read, from the body language of some congregational leaders, a more intense version of the first three points: "We want people to come to church and to sit and listen. We want people to come to Sunday school and to sit and listen. We want people to come to other programs we put on for them and to sit and listen." From what we know about the emerging postmodern generation, we can recognize one reason why this game plan is less effective today: Raised on Nintendo and accustomed to interacting and participating, they do not attend church and sit and listen because they do not voluntarily attend anything and sit and listen. Even newspaper cartoons, such as "Slylock Fox," are becoming interactive!

That traditional model will vary slightly from one congregation, denomination, or tradition to another. Some churches no longer expect people, at least not adults, to attend Sunday school. Some churches, such as the Roman Catholic Church, expect people to attend the confessional (the rough equivalent of Protestant pastoral care). So we observe some variations within the model, but most traditional churches practice their version of the model without questioning its validity and assume that the inherited model would still build the kind of people they believe

God wants if only they tried harder. I cannot share their confidence, because Old East Side's way of doing church is no longer producing its fair share of apostles, prophets, saints, and martyrs anywhere I have been able to find.

(I have inferred this traditional paradigm for "doing church" from studying traditional North American Protestant churches. Undoubtedly, churches in other traditions of world Christianity "do church" by different paradigms that, to my knowledge, no one has yet studied to make explicit. One contrasting paradigm is shared by most of the "state churches" of Western and Eastern Europe. The main business of those churches, in addition to perpetuating their revered traditions, is to serve the people of their extensive "parishes," primarily by providing the rites of passage—baptisms, weddings, and funerals—for their people. One commentator once observed that most European Christians go to church only three times in their life, and they are unconscious all three times! Which is not quite fair, because they often attend other people's baptisms, weddings, and funerals. Another commentator once observed that, any case, the paradigm focuses on getting people "hatched, matched, and dispatched!" Which is not quite fair, because many European state churches also train children for confirmation and, say, provide counseling for couples seeking more glue for their marriages; so they get people hatched, attached, matched, patched, and dispatched! This model, too, fails to produce a laity who engages in ministry and outreach; but, in contrast to most North American Protestant churches, most European state churches do not purport to produce such a laity.)

So the first reason that Old East Side's way is impotent is that pre-Christian people experience the church as culturally irrelevant. The church's members intuitively know that their unchurched friends cannot relate to Old East Side's style, language, liturgy, and music; so they do not even consider inviting them.

Recovering a More "Apostolic Way" of "Doing Church"

Samuel Shoemaker's haunting question, posed a half century ago, has never been more compelling: "Can your kind of church change this kind of world?" When consulting with church leaders, I sometimes ask that question, and then, saying nothing more, I wait for them to deal with it. Shoemaker's question has become inescapable. Occasionally, I find it useful to retreat into a "compromised" version of the question: "Can your kind of church even *engage* this kind of world?"

Fortunately (or providentially) a contrasting, and more "apostolic," way of "doing church" is available. The apostolic way is rooted and modeled in very early Christianity. Christian movements, such as the Celtic, Wesleyan, and Pentecostal movements, that once strived to recover the ancient apostolic mission, essentially recovered the apostolic way of doing church as well. This perennial model for "the apostolic congregation" has a set of core perspectives that have proved remarkably adaptable to an incredibly wide range of historical and cultural contexts. Most important, the apostolic way of doing church produces the kind of proactive, compassionate, ministering, witnessing laity that proponents of the 1957 model want to produce but cannot. (For instance, in 1995, a polling organization surveyed the membership of The Community Church of Joy, a Lutheran church in Glendale, Arizona. Of Joy's six thousand members, 81 percent reported inviting at least one person within the past year, and 18 percent had invited seven or more.)

Two of the many specific features of an apostolic perspective—(a) cultural relevance and (b) lay ministries—appear to be the 20 percent that accounts for about 80 percent of the difference.[4] We feature "cultural relevance" in this chapter, and an "empowered laity" in the next chapter.

Most informed Christians know that if a dozen of us from Old East Side Church served as an "apostolic team" to serve and reach a tribe of Aymara Indians in the steppes of Bolivia, we would plant a culturally Aymara church. We would not expect, much less require, the host population to learn English; we would learn and speak the Aymara dialect of the people. We would not force eighteenth-century German pipe organ music on the people; we would encourage the development of an indigenous Christian music, using Aymara musical instruments, rhythms, and melodies. We would not try to build a church patterned after the sending church back in New Jersey; any church facility would reflect indigenous Aymara architecture.

If we are typical "Old East Siders," however, it has never occurred to us that an "indigenous" mission approach is now as important for a North American mission field as for a South American (or African or Asian) mission field. Old East Side's leaders have not yet discovered the fact that, among pre-Christian peoples, the interest in eighteenth-century German pipe organ music is not much more epidemic in North America than in South America! Most churches do not yet realize that, to reach more of the 150 million secular people in the American mission field, it is necessary to express the Christian faith in ways that are culturally appropriate to them. The ways we have traditionally done church seem so natural to us that we assume everyone ought to resonate with the style, language, aesthetics, and music that we are used to, and if they don't, there is something wrong with them!

In the 1960s and the 1970s, a few church leaders realized that the people they had an opportunity to reach would not, and probably could not, respond to language and music they did not understand. They pioneered more "contemporary" worship, they developed "seeker-sensitive services" and then "seeker-driven services," and they were "shot at" by many traditional church leaders. Gradually, however, a paradigm shift spread across the land. Today, in cities, perhaps 1 in 6 churches offers a "contemporary" service in addition to the traditional service. More and more churches, but still a small minority, offer *only* contemporary services. Furthermore, the trend that I identified in 1996, the emergence of apostolic congregations, is now accelerating:

The apostolic congregations emerging over the land are different from the traditional churches more on this (cultural) point than on any other. As the apostle Paul was willing to "become all things to all people that [he] might by all means save some," so *we are observing the emergence of entire congregations who are willing to be culturally flexible in order to reach people.* The churches are dramatizing a truth that missionaries have known for decades: To reach pre-Christian populations, it is necessary for a church to become culturally indigenous to its "mission field"—whether in Asia, Africa, Latin America, Oceania, Europe, or North America. When a church employs the language, music, style, architecture, art forms, and other forms of the target population's culture, Christianity then has a fair chance to become contagious within their ranks. But when the church's communication forms are alien to the host population, they may never perceive that Christianity's God is for people like them.[5]

We saw in chapter 1 that Paul advised the Christian movement in Corinth to adapt to the language and culture of the peoples of that city and province (1 Cor. 9). This was not merely Paul's preferred policy; the principle of "indigenous ministry" had been validated at the Jerusalem Council (reported in Acts 15). At a practical level, an "indigenous strategy" involves speaking the people's language—even their dialect or "heart language"—communicating the gospel's meaning through their aesthetics and music, and cooperating with their customs. At a deeper level, indigenous ministry involves engaging the attitudes, beliefs, and values characteristic of the society, especially the core attitudes, beliefs, and values that shape the "worldview lens" through which they view life and the world.

Insights for an "Indigenous Strategy"

Though every church leader in any mission field should have a working knowledge of "Cultural Anthropology 101," several major insights have helped church leaders understand the rationale for an indigenous strategy.

A viable understanding begins with an informed understanding of "culture." People in one society characteristically behave, live, feel, think, and see the world very differently from the people in a different society, and the concept of "culture" is the best cognitive category available to make sense of these differences and to inform more effective communication between societies. For example, a young woman recently visited her older brother who is employed in Morocco. A local sheik offered her brother six thousand camels if he could marry the young woman. (On the game show *Jeopardy*, she reported that the sheik's opening bid was five thousand camels, but her brother was holding out for ten thousand!) You account for this intercultural incident, and thousands of others, only by understanding something about cultural differences.

Craig Storti, building on more than three hundred published definitions of culture, offers this useful definition: "Culture is the shared assumptions, values, and beliefs of a group of people which result in characteristic behaviors."[6] His definition is useful because it shows that a culture is analogous to an iceberg: partly visible (behaviors) and substantially invisible (assumptions, values, and beliefs). It also shows that, very frequently, there is a causal relation between the part under the surface and the things people do and say that are sometimes visible, but not always.

Whether a society's people transport themselves and their goods by camel, llama, ox, or horse may be dictated more by climate and topography than by any deep beliefs or values. Whether people eat with chopsticks or with a knife and fork, or drive their cars on the left or the right, may represent precedents rooted in mere historical accidents. We do thousands of things—but not everything—the way we do them because of our "cultural script." For instance, the peoples of the earth do many things similarly because they share a common human nature. Furthermore, people are individuals, so some things they do are not culturally scripted, but unique to the person. As Sigmund Freud once said, "Sometimes, a cigar is just a cigar," with no deeper (or wider) meaning to be inferred. But, much of how we live and express ourselves "is a direct result of what we assume, value, or believe in."[7]

Understanding culture is important because we live in a vast world of cultures, and more and more cultures, like ancient Corinth, now occupy our cities. Scholars typically identify ten to twelve "macrocultures," or cultural families, across the earth—such as the Nordic, Germanic, Anglo, Latin European, Eastern European, Far Eastern, Near Eastern, Arabic, sub-Sahara African, and Latin American macrocultures. (Each macroculture contains several or more specific cultures. The Latin European macroculture, for instance, includes Belgian, French, Spanish, Italian, and Portuguese cultures.[8]) India and Brazil may be the two nation-states that we can identify as macrocultures, though great numbers of Indians (particularly Tamil Indians) are in diaspora across much of the earth. We can also observe, in addition to specific cultures such as the Tamil or the Italian, a range of subcultures, microcultures, and countercultures, and even regional, generational, and occupational subcultures.

Christian leaders who are uninformed about culture, and the cultures in their ministry area, are malequipped to lead their churches in outreach ministries. Furthermore, the necessity of understanding and adapting to the other culture is much greater in outreach to peoples of other macrocultures. Since we understand people of another subculture within our macroculture more easily than we understand the people of other macrocultures, an Anglo-American church might reach some Australians without much adaptation, and a Spanish-speaking church might even "get lucky" in outreach to some Italians. Effective outreach to peoples of other cultural families within our city, however, requires essentially the same understanding and adaptation that overseas missions would require.

Culture Communicates

The supreme reason why Christians reaching out farther should take culture seriously is that the meaning of the gospel (like the meaning of anything) is communicated in many ways through a culture, *not* through language alone. In the history of Christian mission, leaders have often assumed that it was enough to get the language right, that is, communication is essentially (or only) a translation challenge. One man, however, demonstrated that communication is more complex than that; to his credit, he provided a rough map through the complexity.

He was Edward T. Hall, a pioneering cultural anthropologist. He defined culture as "the silent language."[9] Language, Hall observed, is only one of the "primary message systems" in a culture that communicates meaning (or blocks its communication). Our language is the one communication system within our culture that we learn consciously; from the time we are babies, we learn our language consciously, word by word. So when someone uses words we do not understand, we are quite consciously aware of the communication barrier; "I did not understand those words."

Hall taught us, however, that we also communicate through (at least) nine other "primary message systems" that, in our enculturation, we did not learn consciously like we learned our language; we "acquired" our other primary message systems unconsciously. Most of us, for example, are somewhat aware of the influence of nonverbal communication factors such as touch, facial expressions, eye contact, and gestures; but communication takes place in other ways that most people are less aware of but, nevertheless, affected by. Several of Hall's primary message systems are virtually as important in communicating Christianity as language and, together, are probably more important.

For instance, Hall observed a primary message system he called "territoriality"; *space*, and how we use it, communicates. For instance, you can stand too close to a stranger on an elevator and observe the response to an obvious "message." Hall points out that the culturally "normal space," or personal distance, between two persons in conversation is much less in Latin America than in North America. When a North American and a Latin American are in conversation, they each tend to stand about the "right" distance from each other; but the Latin American will experience the North American (who keeps backing up) as "distant," and the North American will experience the Latin American (who keeps inching forward) as "pushy"—*unless* one of them knows to *adapt* to the cultural expectation of the other. More profound, all creatures— from amoebas, bees, birds, cats, and eagles, to humans— need their "space"; its loss, or the threat of its loss, can induce pathology. Much human conflict over the ages, including the Middle Eastern conflict today, is about space and what space means to people and peoples. Some Christian traditions seem to be more aware than others of how space communicates and the power of "sacred space." I once sensed some of that power while standing at the grave of Saint Patrick in Downpatrick, Ireland.

Again, Hall observed a primary message system he called "temporality"; *time,* and how we use it, communicates. For instance, you communicate something by arriving for an appointment early, and something else by arriving late. Hall noticed that "late" is defined differently in different societies. More profound, he observed that some cultures are "monochronic"—they tend to do one thing at a time—and others are "polychronic"—they do several things concurrently, such as listening to music, socializing, greeting passersby, and feasting, while doing business. Some Christian traditions know how to do worship for polychronic societies; for instance, people come and go and it is no big deal, their music has much more "going on" concurrently, and their liturgy features more improvisation and spontaneity and engages more of the senses. Again, some Christian traditions milk the liturgical church year for enormously more meaning than other traditions.

Hall identified "play" as one of the ten primary message systems. He observed that play, in some form(s), is expressed in all human cultures and in many animal species. Any culture's "play" system illustrates how the primary message systems are "intertwined"; so, for instance, in any culture there are places for play and times for play, and much "learning" (another primary message system) is experienced through play. Some churches seem to take the "play" message system seriously; their worship is often enjoyable, much Christian education takes place through games and simulations, and their life together is more "fun" than the people at Old East Side would think "proper."

Hall also observed that much meaning is communicated through "materials." For instance, he observed (before Marshall McLuhan) that we develop material "extensions"—such as clothes, furniture, building, and weapons—for almost everything we do with our bodies; and that material, and how we use it, communicates. There is a modest literature, for instance, on the "rhetoric of clothing"—the "dress for success" articles serving as a superficial example. Hall also observed that we extend ourselves through "media," which, depending on the culture, might be smoke signals, drums, letters, books, radio, television, or E-mail. Visual material "symbols" are also capable of communicating in powerful ways. The fish and the cross have long been employed as Christian symbols; and, periodically, Christianity has known how to harness the visual, creative, and performing arts to communicate Christian truth. Many Western Protestant churches today, however, still rely on language to carry all the freight; but for postmodern, right-brained, multisensory populations, language alone is not likely to mediate the full revelation.

Form and Meaning

"Form" and "meaning" are the most important key terms in understanding how Christian advocates can use cultural understanding to communicate the gospel more effectively. "Meaning," Charles Kraft tells us, "is the structuring of information in the minds of persons."[10] "Form" refers to the culture's observable customs and products. Kraft draws upon Louis Luzbetak in suggesting that the "meaning" of a particular form within a culture "consists of 'the totality of subjective associations attached to the form.' "[11] A given form—from a word such as *love*, to a visual symbol such as a Celtic cross, to a ritual action such as the Eucharist—can stimulate more than one meaning in people's experience, and a given meaning may be conscious or subconscious. In effective ministry, especially evangelism, we communicate the gospel's meaning through forms that are culturally "indigenous," rather than culturally "foreign," to the target population.

The "form" and "meaning" categories make clear that, essentially, we have only four options in reaching a population; and, based on many generations of cross-cultural mission experience, we can predict the likely outcome for each option.

One option, for instance, is to employ indigenous forms to communicate indigenous meanings. In such a case, nothing changes. The people's traditional religion, worldview, and lifestyle remain intact; indeed, they are reinforced. For many traditional religions, this means that evil forces still victimize the people and they still believe that the High God is inaccessible.

A second option is to persuade the people to adopt "foreign" forms, such as Western Christian art, architecture, saints, and holidays, without changing the meanings with which the people interpret transcendence. The outcome is a Syncretism, or "Christo-paganism," in which the forms appear Christian to a Western outsider, but, in the experience of the nationals, the old meanings of the traditional religion are retained. As one of many possible examples, the name of a Western saint may simply function as the new name for a god or goddess in the traditional religion. Many Roman Catholic leaders are concerned about the traditional meanings that their people attach to the European Catholic forms that were introduced in the colonial period of Catholicism's mission to South America. (The popular religion of North America, in which millions of people believe in "luck," "karma," American chauvinism, *and* Jesus, is also "a tad" syncretistic.)

A third option is to communicate foreign meanings through foreign Christian forms. The outcome is Foreign Christianity. The first generation of converts, particularly those close to the missionaries, may understand enough of the Christian faith to constitute a viable church; but the second or third generation typically slides into Syncretism. Across the U.S.A., churches like Old East Side that are still trying to make seventeenth-century European Christianity work in twenty-first-century America are experienced (or ignored) as examples of Foreign Christianity.

The fourth, and preferred, option is to communicate the "foreign" gospel through indigenous forms, which results in Indigenous Christianity. (The gospel is "foreign" in the sense that it had to be revealed by God to the human race, and that revelation extends, culture by culture, through cross-cultural ministry. Nevertheless, the earth's peoples usually experience the gospel as congruent with some of their beliefs, experiences, and aspirations, since Jesus Christ comes "not to destroy, but to fulfill.")

Without gross oversimplification, we can "chart" these four options:

1. Indigenous meanings + indigenous forms = Traditional Religion
2. Indigenous meanings + foreign forms = Syncretism
3. Foreign Christian meanings + foreign forms = Foreign Christianity
4. Foreign Christian meanings + indigenous forms = Indigenous Christianity

The Periodic Loss and Recovery of Indigenous Christianity

The indigenous approach to the peoples of the earth was modeled in Jesus' ministry, authorized by the Jerusalem Council, modeled by the apostles' ministries, mandated in 1 Corinthians, and enabled the faith's spread to many peoples across the Mediterranean world. Nevertheless, church leaders have often been oblivious to the meaning and importance of this missionary principle. More often than not, church leaders have too closely identified the Christian faith with the forms in which they received it, or the style, language, aesthetics, and music they are used to. When the church has engaged in mission without distinguishing between form and meaning, it has usually insisted that new populations adopt the forms, even the language, of the "sending church."

The problem began early. The Jerusalem church assumed that circumcision, kosher food, and other Jewish customs should be required for everyone who followed Jesus as the Messiah. Though their team lost the vote at the Jerusalem Council, many of them did not change their minds. Indeed, they launched their own mission to much of the Roman Empire. The mission of the "Judaizers" probably reached Egypt and several other regions to which Paul never ventured. Their mission preceded, or followed, Paul's in several cities; they energized the legalism with which Paul contended in his letter to the Galatians. Vincent Donovan explains: "The Judao-Christians thought they could convert the world of the pagan Roman Empire on their own terms."[12] They seem to have assumed, Donovan contends, that the Gentile cultures and religions were darkness only, with no point of contact with the gospel, with nothing in their language or culture that could help interpret the gospel, with no prevenient action of God in their religion; so "they saw no need for cross-culturation. They were blinded to the fact that they had trapped Christ in their culture."[13] The Jewish Christian mission was a force for two generations, but, Donovan tells us, "because they made no efforts at cross-culturation, they died. After A.D. 140 there is not a trace of them left in the world of living human beings."[14]

So the Hellenistic branch of the Church, speaking the people's *koine* Greek and adapting to many cultures, prevailed across the Mediterranean world and won the majority of the urban peoples of an empire by persuasion alone. The Church, however, did not learn sufficiently from this history, and, over the centuries, the "cultural imperialists" have been in control at least as much as the "indigenizers." Church history provides more examples than we can cite here, but three sagas are worth retelling.

As the Roman Empire displaced the Hellenist Empire, and Latin became the predominant language of government, commerce, and the Church, in time the Church regarded Latin, and Roman ways of "doing church," as normative for all Christians. With this shift, the Church did less mission, and the peoples they did reach were already "Romanized" or were expected to become culturally Roman. "Once any society accepted Christianity, the politically dominant Roman wing of the Church insisted that the young churches organize in the Roman pattern of dioceses led by bishops and learn to worship in Latin, follow the liturgy from Rome, sing the music from Rome, etc."[15] Peoples who could not be reached through the Latin language and Roman forms, and were not eager to be reinculturated, were "barbarians" and assumed to be unreachable.

The unreachable peoples of Europe might never have been reached without the daring imagination of a man named Patrick. When Patrick was a very young man, an Irish tribe enslaved him for six years. While a slave, Patrick became articulate in the Gaelic language, came to understand the people and their ways, and began imagining ways they might be reached. He escaped to Europe, acquired a theological education, and served as a priest in England. Years later, he believed he was called through a dream to take the gospel to the Irish; with the initial backing of the Church of England and from the papacy, Patrick returned to Ireland with an apostolic team in A.D. 432. They itinerated for twenty-eight years, and the north half of Ireland became substantially Christian; the rest of Ireland was reached within another two generations. This movement reached the Irish through their own Gaelic language and through the music, arts, and other forms of their culture. Patrick's movement, geographically beyond the controlling reach of Rome, had reinvented Indigenous Christianity.

Engaging in further strategic adaptations, the movement sent Columba to reach the Picts of Scotland, and Aidan to reach the Anglo-Saxons that had swarmed England, and Columbanus to launch multiple movements to reach many "barbarian" peoples of continental Europe. In time, they reached much of Europe—by reaching many barbarian peoples thought impossible to reach! They planted indigenous forms of Christianity everywhere. Although impressed with these movements, Rome found them difficult to control and could not affirm "doing church" in ways that deviated from Rome's preferred way. In the Synod of Whitby in A.D. 664, Rome began the process of forcing the movement-oriented Celtic wing of the Church into compliance with the stagnant Roman wing of the Church. It took another two centuries to enforce compliance everywhere; but by then, most of Europe had been reached and the reproductive power of the indigenous principle had been widely demonstrated once again.[16]

The "our way is best" syndrome is a creative pathology; it takes many different forms. Whatever the form, the pre-Christian people who do not already share in the "stained glass culture" usually experience the Church, saying, "It's my way, or the highway," and the people usually take the highway. In eighteenth-century England, the established Church of England spoke the same national language and shared the same general culture as the unchurched masses who crowded into the cities during the Industrial Revolution. The Church, however, spoke "proper English," regular attendees had mastered a "church etiquette," and, in many ways, it reeked of an elitist subculture within the general culture. The Church may as well have spoken Latin. "Superior" dialects and forms can be more alienating than foreign languages and forms. Many Anglican leaders assumed that the "common people" were hopeless and impossible to Christianize.

Throughout much of his life, John Wesley had interacted with prisoners, poor people, and other common people, enough so to feel their alienation from the Anglican Church and to infer its causes. In 1738, he launched a "Methodist" movement within the Church of England that was intended to serve as a lay apostolic and renewal order within the Church of England; the movement's major expressions reflected Indigenous Christianity two centuries before cultural anthropologists told us what to call it.

For instance, Methodism began, in every city, by identifying with people on their turf through ministry and conversation, and through open-air field-preaching where the people gathered—such as a town square. The movement built chapels that reflected an indigenous church architecture, in which people felt comfortable. Wesley's brother Charles led the way in producing an indigenous Christian music; Charles wrote poetry to be sung to the music the people were culturally shaped to understand—often the music sung in public houses. Wesley encouraged his leaders to communicate Christian meaning through the common language of unchurched people and to avoid "quaint" expressions and "peculiar" language. Wesley warned his movement about the dangers of ever being experienced as "sophisticated." Through an indigenous approach, early Methodism reached tens of thousands of the "impossible to reach" people in Wesley's own lifetime and, under Francis Asbury's leadership, duplicated the achievement in the American colonies. The Church of England was not impressed, much less educable, and eventually forced Methodism to separate from the Church in which Wesley was ordained until his death.[17]

By the late–nineteenth century, the "colonial" period of Christian mission had produced some version of the "cultural imperialism" problem on every inhabited continent. Despite the experiments, modeling, and advocacy of brilliant culturally aware leaders such as Robert de Nobili, Matteo Ricci, John Wesley, Rufus Anderson, Henry Venn, William Taylor, and Roland Allen, most missions assumed most of the time that the forms favored by educated Western Christian leaders should be used everywhere. So, as one example among very many, the seventeenth-century Puritan mission to Native American Indians isolated converts into

Christian towns and their children into Christian boarding schools, because the missionaries felt compelled to "civilize" Indians "according to the British model."[18] Even in Western countries, the state churches and mainline denominations were employing an elitist left-brained "rational" approach to "civilizing" the "less-cultured" people.

The most obvious response to the cultural imperialism of Western churches and missions has been the worldwide Pentecostal movement. The movement began in 1906 among urban, down-and-out, disenfranchised, unlettered African American, Hispanic, and Anglo people in the now-famous Azusa Street Revival in Los Angeles. Within a year, it spread to every continent; it grew from nothing to over 400 million people in less than a century. It stands, today, as a contagious alternative to the historic denominations almost everywhere. It has contrasted establishment rationalist Christianity with a people's religion of the heart. It has contrasted the educated Western way of doing church with an astonishing creative freedom in adapting to local cultures and needs. Harvey Cox reports that

> the movement raced across the planet with . . . electrifying speed. Its potent combination of biblical imagery and ecstatic worship unlocked existing, but often repressed religious patterns, enabling Pentecostalism to root itself in almost any culture. Not only did missionaries travel all over the globe (thirty-eight left from Azusa Street within six months of the mission's origin), but wherever they went, the people who heard them seemed to make the message their own and fan out again. Almost instantly Pentecostalism became Russian in Russia, Chilean in Chile, African in Africa. Within two years the movement had planted itself in fifty countries. It was a religion made to travel, and it seemed to lose nothing in the translation.[19]

The Pentecostal movement's aggressive openness to different cultures now stands as a monumental challenge, almost everywhere, to the elitist, rationalistic, anal-retentive

state churches and mainline denominations that still confine the expression of the gospel's meaning to their inherited Western forms. Nowhere is this more apparent than in
the contrasting policies regarding music. The hundreds of
thousands of churches like Old East Side still rely on traditional European church music played (preferably) on a pipe
organ, with the possible addition of a trumpet on Easter
Sunday. Most Pentecostal churches, notice, "gladly welcome any instrument you can blow, pluck, bow, bang,
scrape, or rattle in the praise of God. . . . Nor . . . is there any
style of music that is deemed irredeemably profane by
Pentecostals."[20]

Top Ten Insights Supporting Culturally Relevant Christianity

Once we know something about culture and the primary
message systems and meaning and form and the church's
repeated struggle to recover the strategy of indigeneity, we
are ready to consider the "Top Ten Insights Supporting
Culturally Relevant Christianity."

10. Cultural relevance is the rationale for "contempo-
    rary worship." Most of us who advocate culturally
    current approaches to church leadership, liturgy, and
    music do not have a bias to, much less an obsession
    for, novelty. Our understanding of Christianity and
    the purpose of its mission is quite "classical." We are
    not trendy, *avant garde*, with-it kind of people. We
    have observed, however, that the church's commu-
    nication forms need to facilitate, rather than frus-
    trate, the communication of the gospel's meaning to
    outsiders.
9. Contrary to what most church leaders have heard, *all*
    worship services are "contemporary"! The problem is

that most of the worship services in churches like Old East Side are "contemporary" to some other culture, or some prior generation, or both. Without doubt, the traditional church was once wonderful and still serves traditional church members who have strong roots in the past. The challenge and opportunity, however, is to shape liturgy and church life in ways indigenous to the cultures in the community, in this generation.

8. Cultural relevance is one way we extend Incarnational Christianity. Jesus' original incarnation involved adapting to ("hillbilly") Aramaic-speaking, first-century, Galilean, Jewish culture. His Body, the Church, is called to adapt to the tongue and culture of the people beyond the Church's walls in every generation.

7. Employing culturally relevant forms is desirable because God's revelation usually, and best, breaks through to people through their own language and the other forms of their culture. From almost twenty centuries of Christian mission, this is our most obvious insight: God's revelation is much less likely to break through when packaged in culturally alien forms; God's revelation is much more likely to break through when presented in culturally indigenous forms. Their culture is the preferred medium of God's self-revelation to every people.

6. When the missionary congregation expresses the gospel in the cultural forms of the receptor population, they are much more likely to perceive that Christianity is for "people like us." Once the congregation reaches a critical mass of the target population, it is positioned to become a local movement, because when seekers come to church, they are often asking two questions: (1) "Is this faith for people like me?" (That is the indigeneity question.) and (2) "Do any

people like me go to this church?" (That is the identi-fication question.) They get their answers from the people and cultural cues they observe.

5. Most traditional churches in the U.S.A. have already come a very long way—in agreeing that ministry in the people's *language* is necessary to reach them. In the 1950s or the 1960s, Old East Side Church dropped such language as "thee" and "thou" from its liturgical language and quietly, without fanfare, shifted from the King James translation of the Scripture to the Revised Standard translation or some other culturally current translation. In the same period, the Roman Catholic Church dropped the Latin requirement for its churches. Although we still need to work on lesser problems, such as churchy jargon and the "stained glass voice," the major battle over language has been won—without the victory ever being officially declared.

4. Traditional churches like Old East Side, however, have not yet discovered that culture is "the silent language." As we saw from Edward T. Hall's studies of cultures, language is only one of the ten (or so) pri-mary message systems in a culture that communi-cates meaning (or blocks its communication). The strategic church will learn to use time, space, symbols, music, architecture, the arts, and even play to com-municate Christianity's meaning to all the senses.

3. Furthermore, traditional churches do not yet per-ceive how deeply culture shapes personality and worldview, that culture is no less than "the software of the mind." That metaphor from the world of com-puters, contributed by Dutch cultural anthropologist Geert Hofsted's *Culture's Consequences*, takes the place of the analogy for culture we never had before! All people have the same "hardware"; the DNA sim-ilarity between all the earth's peoples exceeds 99

percent. Our respective cultures, however, have given us something like thirty thousand distinct softwares. Now, we know that two computers have no difficulty communicating with each other *if* they share the same software. However, if Computer B's software is even slightly different from Computer A's software, even if they have different "generations" of the same software, some data can get lost or garbled in transmission. And if two different softwares inhabit our two computers, you can forget communication—unless one of the computers has added some software making translation possible. Culture is more profound, and culture differences go much deeper, than the usual categories, such as "diversity," suggest. So, unless the church adapts to the target population's "software," the people may not "get it."

2. Since most church leaders do not yet know that culture is "the silent language" and "the software of the mind," they usually resist making the changes needed to "do church" in ways that fit the culture of an unchurched population. Indeed, most church leaders do not yet distinguish, conceptually, between meaning and form, so they assume that perpetuating the old forms is necessary to be faithful to the gospel. Some church leaders seem to believe that the Western church's inherited aesthetic is superior, so they see their main business as "improving" or "lifting" other people culturally!

1. Consequently, most traditional "culturally irrelevant" churches cannot reach, and retain, pre-Christian people in significant numbers. Indeed, as we saw, Old East Side Church cannot even retain a bare majority of its own young people. There is, however, some good news buried in this report. Some churches are not open to the changes necessary to reach outsiders, but

they are open to the changes necessary to keep their own youth. Our youth are washed by the same cultural sea changes that influence secular people, so the changes that would help us engage our own young people are essentially the same needed to reach secular people. While we still have them, our youth are the bicultural confederates who can help us identify the changes needed to move from tradition to mission.

FECs (Frequently Expressed Challenges)

In the years that I have "encouraged" churches to adopt an indigenous strategy to reach people, this theme has met far more resistance, and hostility, than any of the other strategic themes related to evangelization. The following "challenges" are typical, both in substance and in the visceral style of today's challengers to the principle of cultural relevance.

"We are not going to change what we do every six months just to keep up with the top 20 songs and every other fad in American pop culture."

The challenger *might* change her mind upon considering some important distinctions related to time and space, and between "popular" culture and "traditional" culture. "Popular" culture varies little across space; much of the same music and clothing fashions are prominent in, say, Chicago, Tokyo, Sao Paulo, and Moscow. Popular culture, however, changes a great deal over time. The changes in popular culture, which are often called "fads," are short lived. This year's "hit" will not be next year's.

Traditional culture, compared to popular culture, varies a great deal across space. The cultural differences between the earth's fourteen or fifteen "macrocultural regions," such as between the Arabic and the North American macrocultures, are enormous. Even within a macroculture, the traditional cultural differences are often large—as between New England, Appalachia, and the American Southwest. Traditional cultures change much slower than popular cultures, but they do change over time. Changes within traditional cultures are called "trends."

Old East Side Church is experienced as culturally irrelevant, not because it doesn't stampede after every popular fad, but because the church has not even flexed with the much slower trends of the surrounding traditional culture. Although some effective youth ministries monitor, and adapt to, some of the popular culture's changing fads, cultural relevance for most churches means adapting to the glacierlike trends of the traditional culture.

> "Our church refuses to compromise the gospel by being co-opted by the culture."

This detractor points to a real danger. Some churches do "accommodate" to, and become indistinguishable from, their culture. The Church of England, for instance, is labeled "the Tory party at prayer." Churches, however, that understand the distinction between form and meaning are seldom vulnerable to this danger. Furthermore, churches that understand the indigenous principle, by which we use the culture's forms to communicate the gospel's meaning, tend to be the churches reaching pre-Christian populations.

The detractor alerts us to another danger—compromising the gospel. The gospel, however, is entrusted to us to communicate it. As God sends the rain and snow to water the earth to grow grain for bread, so God also sends his Word to "accomplish that which I purpose" (Isa. 55:11). In other words, if the gospel is presented in a way that lost people are not likely to "get it," the gospel has been compromised.

> "The traditional service we offer now serves a satisfied con-
> gregation, and they pay the bills. If we changed that
> service, burned the organ, and featured electric guitars and
> drums, we would lose our base of support."

I understand. Actually, we seldom have compelling reasons to dump a traditional service (or any service) that has
a congregation supporting it. The best strategy, in every
growth opportunity, is to *add* services that reach different
slices of humanity. One day, in the foreseeable future,
many urban churches will feature (say) two traditional
services, a sacramental service, two contemporary services
(one Saturday evening, the other Sunday morning), a
"signed" service for deaf people, a jazz service, a soft rock
service, a recovery service, and Spanish, Swahili, and
Tongan language services. Each service would feature a
different liturgy and music, each shaped by its own lay
worship team, with a version of the same homily in each
service.

> "The idea of having a second, liturgically different worship
> service is such an unprecedented and radical idea that we
> could never sell it to our people."

Five words come to mind, and the five words are: "tom-
myrot," "horse-feathers," "fiddlesticks," "rubbish," and
"balderdash." It is *not* a radical idea, and we have more
precedent for variety than uniformity. For instance, many
of our churches first worshiped in the European language
of an immigrant population and later added an English-
language service. Moreover, most of our churches once had
a "seeker service" called the Sunday evening service; it
was, for its time, a culturally relevant service for introduc-
ing Christianity to pre-Christian people. Today's culturally
relevant services are, philosophically, in continuity with
the old Sunday evening service. So we have more precedent for liturgical variety than for liturgical uniformity.

CHAPTER FOUR

Apostolic Ministry Through an Empowered Laity

T he previous chapter profiled the hypothetical Old East Side Church to dramatize the paradigm shift necessary to move from tradition to mission in the emerging "Corinthian" future. Old East Side, historically, is the product of the Christian world mission. Once, some missionaries cared enough and dared enough to reach the European ancestors of the people who now attend Old East Side; and the first converts, back in Scotland or Sweden or Switzerland, reached out to their people; and the movement then became contagious. When Old East Side's European forebears crossed the Atlantic Ocean to North America, they followed the immigration patterns of "our people," but they also saw

North America as a vast mission field that needed to be reached.

Slowly, very slowly, the priority shifted from retaining our mobile people and reaching other people, to caring for our settled people and preserving the tradition and institution. The descendants of the people once reached by the mission, and who extended the mission, have not been in serious mission for decades. In the 1960s and 1970s, they fueled their denial by saying, "Everything we do is mission!" That pretense was quietly abandoned, and, ever since, some of the people have wondered what it would take to reach people and change lives and be a movement once again. But the church has not engaged in serious outreach within the memory of anyone now attending Old East Side.

We said that Old East Side Church is captured by an unconscious pathology that makes it difficult for the church to produce the kind of Christian disciples it says it wants. The pathology is rooted in a common mental pattern. People in organizations often assume that whatever we are used to is "normal," and whatever we are not used to is probably "abnormal." So, from decades of shared experience, Old East Siders assume, say, that attending church; bringing our offering envelopes; listening to European organ music, handbells, and sermons; attending church programs; welcoming occasional visits from the pastor; saying our prayers; serving on committees; and maybe going to judicatory or denominational meetings and supporting political resolutions are part of "normal Christianity."

The problem is that the growing numbers of people who aren't enculturated "church people," who never acquired a traditional church etiquette, experience the church's equivalent of the 1956 Oldsmobile as abnormal. One source of the problem is generational. The same generation not shopping for obsolete cars is also not buying the prior generation's version of church. (The Oldsmobile case suggests that the problem goes deeper than a mere "image" problem. In the early 1990s, Oldsmobile's marketing people declared, "This is *not* your father's Oldsmobile!" Younger people visited their local Olds dealer. As they viewed its lines, kicked the tires, studied the instrument panel, and took it for a test drive, it sure felt more like their father's Oldsmobile than they'd been led to expect. So the Oldsmobile division of General Motors is now history.)

Another source of the problem is cultural. The cultures of the peoples of America are, increasingly, not like the seventeenth- or eighteenth-century European culture that the denomination came from, or like the culture of the Eisenhower era, in which the denomination last thrived. So the previous chapter exposed Old East Side's cultural conservatism and made a case for rediscovering the ancient apostolic principle of culturally relevant, "indigenous" Christianity for today's Western mission fields. This chapter features another known key to an apostolic renaissance.

The Early Christian Lay Movement

The early Christianity that exploded across the Judean hills and won an empire by persuasion alone was a lay movement. I once observed a "teachable moment" in which a large Presbyterian audience was reminded of this fact. Jack Rogers, who taught at Fuller Theological Seminary (and is now Moderator of the General Assembly of the Presbyterian Church, U.S.A.), was the speaker. At one point in his address, Rogers spoke, briefly but favorably, of the ordination of women. In the question and answer session, an aggressive fellow on the back row challenged the speaker "to justify the ordination of women, biblically." No one present that day will ever forget Jack Rogers's response: "I will be glad to justify the ordination of women biblically, when I hear *you* justify the ordination of *men*, biblically. I will settle for the ordination of *anyone*, biblically! Early Christianity was *a lay movement. No one* was 'ordained' in the sense that any Christian tradition means it today." Rogers explained that the ordination of some people to the priesthood is a postcanonical development within the Church. It is a product of the Traditions, not of the New Testament.[1]

Rogers was essentially right, of course. Neither Jesus, his disciples, nor his later apostles ever met the educational and ecclesiastical requirements that would have credentialed them to be Jewish priests. The early Christian movement appears to have expanded and developed, for a century at least, without relying upon a set-apart priesthood. God's new people, as a body, constituted a "holy" and "royal priesthood" (1 Pet. 2:4, 9). According to Paul, the Holy Spirit "gifts" all Christians for ministry; specifically, the Spirit gifts some people to be apostles, and others prophets, teachers, miracle workers, healers, helpers, administrators, evangelists, pastors, and other roles, "to equip the saints for the work of ministry, for building up the body of Christ" (see 1 Cor. 12:28 and Eph. 4:11-12). So, there are many ministries, and everyone is gifted for some ministry. The Body of Christ needs all the ministries, and one ministry is not more important than another. We are "called out" *(ekklesia)* from the world to be a people in ministry to one another, and we are sent out *(apostello)* to be in ministry to the world. The New Testament did not inflict upon us the artificial and tragic split between the clergy and the laity, the professionals and the amateurs, the players and the spectators; that came later.

The Priesthood of All Priests

To my knowledge, we do not know exactly when the shift took place; undoubtedly the time varied from one region to another, perhaps from one city to another. By some time in the third century, however, it seems to have been universally assumed that virtually all the ministry that matters, including evangelism, church planting, and mission to other peoples, is assigned to ordained priests. Later, this paradigm would flex enough to include some nonordained people, such as monks, nuns, and people in the "orders" that emerged; but these people, too, were in full-time vocations in the church's service. For over a thousand years, "regular" laypeople—who farmed or raised children or baked bread or guarded castles for a living—were assumed to have no essential role in ministry or evangelization beyond their own family.

We see this clearly in Richard Fletcher's 500-page opus, *The Barbarian Conversion.*[2] Fletcher, a ranking medievalist, believes that Jesus' Great Commission mandates the Church to offer the faith to all people. One needs, he remarks, "only a slight acquaintance with the history of the past 2,000 years to show that Christians have not always heeded even the least ambiguous of instructions!"[3] Indeed, from the second century on, no church leader until Saint Patrick (in the fifth century) appears to have been possessed by deep convictions about the priority of "teaching all nations" and "fishing" for men and women.[4] Until Pope Celestine commissioned Patrick to evangelize the Irish (c. 432), the Church, in the period of the Roman Empire, never appointed a single bishop to venture beyond the Empire's frontier to reach a pagan population.

In that lengthy interim, when it did occur to the Church, say, to preach in a new town or to plant a church, it was assumed to be the task of priests. We know that laity sometimes propagated the gospel and "planted" communities of faith, whether the Church expected them to or not! Christians such as traders, diplomats, soldiers, prisoners, and people in cross-cultural marriages sometimes started churches and then asked the bishop to send them a priest.

Apparently, for a thousand years, this was seldom, if ever, considered a "normal" thing for lay Christians to do. Church planting by laity was so little celebrated that the Church has left us virtually no names, no stories, and no information on how they went about it. Often, when the faith spread to a people without being led by an ordained priest, (ordained) church historians attributed such occurrences to a mysterious "seepage" of Christianity. They had difficulty believing that laity, as peddlers, traders, soldiers, slaves, brides, or ambassadors, were actually capable of communicating the gospel.[5] Church administrators often experienced such new churches as "problems"; the bishop was suddenly obligated to find a priest who could go, and outpost churches were more difficult for a bishop to administer and control.

The church did identify, and count on, some lay roles as churches were planted. Most missionaries had a network of family, friends, and patrons who supported them financially. Landowners were sometimes expected to build a chapel for their household, tenants, and dependents. Sometimes, the Christian queen in a "diplomatic marriage" would encourage her husband into the faith, who would then encourage his subjects to receive baptism. In time, in regions such as Gaul, Spain, and the British Isles, the pattern was to reach the king, who would reach his aristocrats, who would reach their people. From this approach, we are sure that many people joined the church more out of expectation or intimidation or rewards, than from an authentic faith response to the gospel. There was a theory behind this sequence. Fletcher reports that

> early medieval missionaries were firm believers in the "trickle-down" effect. The most easily identifiable and consistently pursued element of strategy was the missionaries' choice to work from the top downwards. If you can convert the directing elite then those who are subject to its direction will follow the lead given.[6]

Fletcher views the trickle-down approach as more effective than, I think, the facts warrant. Indeed, Fletcher cites at least one case of a "percolate-up" model (my term), in which a missionary named Ingo reached serfs first, and this influenced the responsiveness of their lords. John Wesley would one day observe that the "religion must not go from the greatest to the least, or the power would appear to be of men." Donald McGavran would later observe, from an extensive number of mission cases, that "the masses" are usually more receptive than "the classes," and that the faith's contagion usually spreads in a society from the lower classes to the middle and upper classes.

The "Celtic" Exception

The history of the Celtic movement, launched by the evangelization of the north half of Ireland by Patrick and his team, which in time spread to Scotland, England, and much of Western Europe, gives us one notable sustained exception to a thousand years of generalizations. The Celtic movement reached so-called "barbarian" peoples, often destitute populations; it was essentially a lay movement, and it prominently included women, who were known to serve within apostolic teams, to plant churches, and, as in the cases of Brigid and Hilda, to lead some of the large monastic communities that served as mission stations. Within several centuries, however, the Church's politically dominant Roman wing forced the Celtic wing into conformity to the Roman way.[7]

For a thousand years, with the notable exception of "Celtic Christianity," the Western church had low expectations for laity in ministry and mission—except for queens, kings, warrior aristocrats, and financial patrons of mission. The master of the house was to see to it that his wife and children learned the catechism, attended mass, and said their prayers; however, any ministry of laity outside the family, including apostolic ministry, was not on Rome's conceptual map. In the late–Middle Ages, evangelical lay movements such as the Waldensians, the Humiliati, and the Franciscans surfaced; they demonstrated, for anyone who had the eyes to see, that laypeople could live devoutly, serve, and evangelize. These laity, however, plunged full time into these movements. There was still no significant role for mothers and midwives, farmers and merchants—except, in time, the Church imposed a "compulsory tithe" upon the laity!

The Priesthood of All Believers—Proposed

Protestants often assume that Martin Luther "fixed" this problem with his doctrine of "the Priesthood of All Believers." The doctrine, though, achieved some of Luther's objectives better than others: (1) Luther was affirming that believers were not dependent upon an ordained priest to mediate their access to God; because Jesus Christ is the one mediator between believers and God, believers had direct access to God. Luther's people did seem substantially to realize this objective. (2) Luther did not believe that the priesthood is the only "Christian vocation," that people doing faithful work in many different roles are also serving in Christian vocations; many people did discover the dignity of their calling. (3) Luther was affirming that believers should not be totally dependent upon a priest to interpret the Scriptures for them; believers should have direct access to the Scriptures. Luther translated the Bible into German and persuaded Gutenberg to publish it; but Luther learned that distribution of Bibles to all the people did not assure a more biblically literate Church. (4) Luther, most explicitly, attached the doctrine to the idea that every Christian is called to be a priest to others;

that noble idea was never widely implemented within Luther's movement. Indeed, neither Lutheran clergy nor Lutheran laity engaged in any notable cross-cultural mission ventures within Luther's lifetime, or for another century.

The idea of the priesthood of the laity, or any ministry of the laity, was not implemented in Protestant Christianity for a very long time and is not widely implemented even today—except in Pentecostal Christianity. The minds of most mainline Protestants, lay and clergy, are "programmed" by a book that most of them have never read. (In many areas of life, books we have never read shape our paradigms. Most people, for instance, have never read Newton's *Principia Mathematica*, but they assume the validity of his "law of gravity" and a mechanistic explanation for the universe's operation. Again, most people have never read Darwin's *The Origin of Species*, but they assume some "evolutionary" understanding for how creatures, including humans, got to where they are today.)

Richard Baxter As Newton and Darwin for Traditional Protestants

Protestant Christianity's equivalent of Darwin's *Origin of Species*—for understanding who we are—*and* Newton's *Principia*—for understanding our place in the scheme of things, and how the (church) world works—is Richard Baxter's *The Reformed Pastor*,[8] first published in 1656, more than a century after Luther's death. Baxter spent a lengthy career as a Puritan leader and the pastor in Kidderminster, England—then a town of about eight hundred homes and two thousand people. Baxter's job description was daunting. With astonishing industry, he served as *every* person's evangelist, catechist, teacher, overseer, counselor, disciplinarian, liturgist, and preacher (Sunday morning and evening); he took it on himself to minister to all sick people and to visit from house to house.

That is also Baxter's job description for every pastor. The pastor's calling is to do, for everyone, most of the ministry that matters. *The Reformed Pastor* has probably shaped Protestant assumptions on these matters more than any other ten books combined—a fact we can attribute to the gold nuggets Baxter scatters throughout its pages. Many of his insights on the pastor's spiritual preparation and the pastor's motives for ministry and the humility, diligence, prudence, patience, and love that the good pastor expresses through ministry, are magnificent. Moreover, so much Scripture pervades the text, and Baxter's own devotion to Christ and his Church so shines through the book's pages that we should not be surprised that it still inspires after almost 350 years.

The only serious problem with Baxter's classic is its major assumption. When Baxter wrote, the Christian priesthood had already modeled vocational narcissism for over a millennium. With clear exceptions including monarchs, politicians, rock stars, "superjocks," and supermodels, priests have exceeded most other vocations in the degree to which they have assumed that the world revolves around what they do. We Protestants cannot say that the early "reformers," including Luther, Calvin, and Baxter, did anything about this, though, at one level, Luther perceived the problem.

So, we can read Baxter on ministry and never discover that the people of God are the salt of the earth and are gifted for ministry. Baxter's paradigm allows laypeople only a negligible involvement in ministry. For instance, "masters of families" should "carry on the work" that the pastor begins with their families. Or, *if* the pastor cannot visit all the new believers to hear them recite the catechism, it is acceptable for a mature Christian to stand in for the pastor in that modest role. Such concessions are few, and

Baxter is oblivious to the idea that ordinary Christians can reach pre-Christian people. Remarkably, Baxter observes that the number of converts that filled his church far exceeded his evangelistic efforts, but he admits, "I scarce knew how."[9] (It's that "seepage" thing again!) Baxter was driven by, but also blinded by, his paradigm—that ordained people do virtually all the ministry that matters—laypeople are essentially spectators.

The Priesthood of All Believers—Implemented!

Eighty years after Baxter published his book, English Methodism based a movement on a very contrasting paradigm: Laypeople do most of the ministry that matters. John Wesley's movement claimed the world as its parish and implemented Luther's "priesthood of all believers." This was, strategically, the supreme reason for Methodism's unprecedented growth as a lay movement.

In *Church for the Unchurched*, I described the way in which Wesley negotiated this paradigm shift over time, and what it meant to his movement:

> John Wesley came to perceive that the Holy Spirit has gifted many lay-people for all sorts of ministries. Within a year or two after his 1738 Aldersgate experience, Wesley had a movement on his hands, with much need for outreach, teaching, ministry, and leadership—with virtually no ordained clergy at his disposal. The only people available were gifted lay-people.
>
> Wesley did not stampede toward the lay solution, but he had experiential warrant for considering it. As an impressionable boy, he had observed for months the undeniable power of a growing Sunday evening ministry of his own mother, Susanna, as up to 200 people assembled in, and outside, her Epworth kitchen. She later influenced John to the conclusion that Thomas Maxfield, and presumably other laypeople, [was] called by God to preach. Early, he

observed the blessing of God attending the ministries and witness of many Methodist laypeople.

So Wesley evolved into the understanding that the Church's ministry to Christians, and to non-Christians, is primarily entrusted to the laity. While several other traditions, including the Church of England, had some laity involved in some ministries and causes, Methodism quickly "out laicized" the other denominations and became essentially a lay movement.

Laypeople did virtually all the ministry that took place in, and out from, every Methodist society. There were class leaders, and band leaders, and other kinds of small group leaders, as well as local preachers and those so-called "assistants" who took de facto charge of societies and circuits—all laypersons. Other laypeople visited sick and hospitalized people; others worked with children and their families; others visited poor people, widows, and single parent families; still others engaged in conversations with undiscipled people and started new classes for seekers.

Wesley did not leave to chance the organization of lay ministries. Leaders selected people for various ministries with care. Each ministry had a "job description." People were "developed" for various roles. Their performance was observed and "coached." Moreover, in Methodism's unique marriage of ministry and evangelism, everyone who ministered also evangelized. Wesley knew what the church growth movement has (re)discovered—that most of the Christians who regularly share their faith are Christians involved in some ministry, and who experience God working through their ministry. So, the priority objective of class leaders, sick visitors and the other laity in ministry was to "save souls."

Of course, the early Methodist societies had preachers, but it would be easy to exaggerate their status and importance. They served "circuits" of several societies, and they itinerated every year or two; in any case, the vast majority of them were nonordained lay preachers. It is true that, in time, ·the preachers—through their annual conference— governed the connection. The laity were not involved in high level ecclesiastical politics, but their time and energy were thereby freed for ministries in societies and communities.

Wesley believed in the movement's, and the people's, possibilities. He challenged his leaders to read, learn, and develop, and he believed they could be the agents for a great movement of the Spirit. Wesley may have overestimated the gifts and capacities of his people; Gordon Rupp once commented that "Wesley's geese were too often swans in his eyes." But a lay movement Methodism was, a Protestant movement that went quite beyond "priesthood of all believers" sloganeering and actually entrusted virtually all the ministry that matters to laypeople. Methodism was a "lay apostolate" before we knew what to call it.[10]

Methodism, as essentially a lay movement, thrived and grew in many lands for more than a century. Then Methodism, at least in the West, changed profoundly. Pastors started desiring education like the Presbyterians and respect like the Episcopalians. In time, Methodism abandoned its distinctive identity as a lay movement, ordained ministry became a "profession," and more and more ministry (including evangelism) shifted into the pastor's job description. The denomination's churches slowly turned inward, toward caring for members and maintaining the church. Methodist clergy and laity today are much more likely to regard their parish as their world than the world as their parish! Nevertheless, historic Methodism stands as one model, historically achieved and enduring for generations, of the ministry and mission of the laity.

The Emerging Revolution in Lay Ministries

Today, most of the people in the mainline denominations assume the Baxter model more than the Wesley model— mainline Methodism included.[11] That is one reason why the so-called mainline denominations are becoming the "sideline," or "old line," denominations. Within these denominations, however, an increasing number of pioneering congregations have affirmed the apostolic agenda, have rejected the Baxter chaplaincy model, and are deploying laity in ministries and outreach in ways that people who are stuck in the 1950s still regard as "impossible."

For instance, Frazer Memorial United Methodist Church in Montgomery, Alabama, involves over seven thousand members in over two hundred lay ministries. Over two hundred lay shepherds provide pastoral care for church members, and other laity tutor inner-city children; pray with callers by telephone; or engage in a wide range of sports ministries, support ministries, recovery ministries, homeless ministries, and ministries in hospitals, nursing homes, prisons, and other community settings.

The six-thousand-member Community Church of Joy, a church of the Evangelical Lutheran Church in America in Glendale, Arizona, offers a range of support groups, recovery groups, and outreach ministries that include Alcoholics Anonymous and Overeaters Anonymous, support groups for people struggling with AIDS or Chronic Fatigue Syndrome, for codependents and diabetics, for people experiencing separation, divorce, job loss, or grief—including Parents of Murdered Children and Survivors of Homicide. A recent survey revealed that 81 percent of the church's members had invited at least one person within the past year; 18 percent had invited seven or more.

Rick Warren, founding pastor of Saddleback Community Church, a Southern Baptist church in Orange County, California, believes that the greatest challenge facing denominational churches is "turning an audience into an army." The church provides a four-hour seminar, during which people discover their SHAPE—an acronym for the Spiritual Gifts, Heart, Abilities, Personality Type, and Experiences through which God has shaped them for ministry. Several thousand members have discovered their

SHAPE and are now serving in the one ministry (out of 150 options) for which they have most been "shaped."[12]

More churches are deploying lay teams for short-term mission experiences than ever before. A team of, say, twenty laypeople digs wells in rural India for three weeks or builds a chapel in the Dominican Republic, while joining indigenous believers in celebrative worship each evening. In this liminal experience, the team members do no harm, they do a little good, they discover who they are, they contract "apostolic fever," and they now see "home" as the mission field they never perceived before. They catalyze their church for new outreach ministries, and they plant churches serving several ethnic-minority language populations, while supporting more full-time missionaries than the church once dreamed of. Art Beals's *When the Saints Go Marching Out* teaches churches how to get involved in world mission, based upon the pioneering of Seattle's University Presbyterian Church.[13] Global Focus leads world mission seminars in many churches (see www.globalfocus.info or, for Methodists, www.worldparish.org).

Mainline Protestants are producing a distinctive, and reproductive, literature informing a renaissance in pastoral care ministries performed by laity. Mel Steinbron pioneered an early approach in the College Hill Presbyterian Church in Cincinnati; in time, a team of lay pastors was serving all the members of one of the Presbyterian Church's largest congregations. Steinbron published his curriculum, *Can the Pastor Do It Alone?* for lay pastoral caregivers. The book teaches people how to PACE their ministry, that is, how to *Pray* daily for their flock, be *Available* to their people, *Contact* them weekly, and *Encourage* their people to live as faithful disciples. Steinbron created an organization of churches that deploy laity in pastoral care and recently published *The Lay-driven Church*.[14]

Leroy Howe retired early from teaching theology and pastoral care at the Perkins School of Theology, Southern

Methodist University, to lead, expand, and learn from a lay pastoral care movement he started at First United Methodist Church in Richardson, Texas. After several years of experience, he published *A Pastor in Every Pew*,[15] which teaches would-be caregivers the five (learnable) traits that win people's trust: empathy, genuineness, respect, hope, and affirmation. The text also schools caregivers in ten skills involved in pastoral care ministry. Howe's most noteworthy contribution is an approach to lay pastoral care ministry "whether the recipient of the care is Christian or not."[16] In non-Western cities, such as Singapore, some mainline Protestant churches are already growing as teams of laity claim high-rise apartments or whole neighborhoods as their "parish." This will be happening soon through churches in Western cities.

On Either Side of the Mainline (Old line, Sideline) Denominations

Though some churches and pioneering thinkers are breaking out of the Baxter paradigm, in which mainline Protestant Christianity is otherwise entrenched, two other expressions of the Christian faith—on "either side" of Protestant Christianity—are light years ahead.

Pentecostal Christianity's deployment of laity substantially accounts for the fact that, less than a century after its global launch from the 1906 Azusa Street Revival, "it is by far the largest non-Catholic grouping, accounting for one in every four Christians. It is also the fastest growing Christian movement on earth."[17] Thirty-eight people visited Azusa Street within the revival's first six months, and, spontaneously, they took the Pentecostal message and vision to every continent. Pentecostal Christianity rediscovered Paul's understanding that the Holy Spirit has given "spiritual gifts" to every believer for some ministry (see Rom. 4, Eph. 4, and 1 Cor. 12) and that every Christian is called to be in ministry. Pentecostal Christianity now deploys ordinary laypeople, including women, more extravagantly in more ministries than any other Christian tradition. Pentecostal Christianity also assumes that every convert is called to be an evangelist and missionary. In recent years, to cite one case, First Assembly of God in Phoenix has become that denomination's most rapidly growing church—reaching people through more than two hundred lay outreach ministries.

David Martin, a ranking sociologist of religion and, for many years, an English Methodist lay preacher, may be the most astute interpreter of Pentecostal Christianity. He sees Pentecostalism as an extension of what Methodism once was—reaching the lower classes, culturally adaptive wherever it spread, offering an experiential faith, believing that "all things are possible," a cultural revolution, and a lay movement claiming the world for Christ. In his latest book, *Pentecostalism: The World Their Parish*,[18] Martin is suggesting in the book's title (and substance) that, although Methodism has deteriorated from a movement into another generic denomination and has become enough of a spent force that it no longer has a serious world mission, someone else has stepped into the void.

The Roman Catholic Church, on the other side of "mainline Protestant churches," experienced a monumental paradigm shift with, and following, the Second Vatican Council (1962–1965). Hans Küng reminds us that, in the early history before the Church developed a hierarchical organization, "every community, indeed every member of a community, had to stand in the 'apostolic succession'—in accordance with the message and action of the apostles. Not just a few people, but the whole church was an apostolic church, as it would be called in the creed."[19] This apostolic ministry role for all of the people of God was submerged for over fifteen hundred years, Küng admits, but Vatican II represented a serious move to restore the central role of local churches, the use of indigenous languages and liturgies, *and* "the priesthood of all believers."

The Vatican II document that most clearly expresses this "restoration" of the ministry and mission of the laity is *Lumen Gentium*. The document makes clear that the mission originally entrusted to the apostles and their churches was to "continue after their death . . . and . . . until the end of the world." The document defines the essence of the apostolic task as "unceasingly to send heralds of the gospel until such time as the infant churches are fully established and can themselves carry on the work of evangelizing." The mission is assigned to every local church, to be carried out primarily through "the lay apostolate"; modern conditions require that the lay apostolate be restored, "broadened, and intensified." "The obligation of spreading the faith is imposed on every disciple of Christ, according to his ability." The latest edition of the *Catechism of the Catholic Church* declares: "The whole Church is apostolic . . . in that she is 'sent out' into the whole world. All members of the Church share in this mission, though in various ways."[20]

Although the mandates of Vatican II have not been universally applied in the world's Roman Catholic churches (and are, in some quarters, resisted), local churches are now free to implement the Council's vision. The story of Holy Family Roman Catholic Church, in Inverness, Illinois, represents what can happen. The Catholic archdiocese discovered they were losing Catholic people who moved to the northwest region of Greater Chicago; some Catholics were joining Willow Creek Community Church. They consulted with the leaders of Willow Creek—to reflect upon what a Roman Catholic variation upon the Willow Creek "seeker church" might look like. In 1993, Father Patrick Brennan accepted pastoral leadership of the young church after heading the Office of Evangelization for the Chicago Archdiocese. You know that "something is up" when you

access the website and observe Holy Family Church pre-
senting itself as "An Evangelical Church in the Roman
Catholic Tradition."

Today Holy Family averages over ten thousand people
in weekend masses, and Brennan is the church's only
ordained priest! Most of the ministry that matters is done
by gifted and trained laypeople. The church is "mission
driven" and "lay driven." Eight laypeople head the
church's "major ministering communities": worship, family life, communications, outreach and social justice, evangelization and catechesis, pastoral care, operations, and
youth. Today, Holy Family's laypeople are engaged in
more than 120 ministries. Many of the ministries represent
the usual range of support, recovery, and social ministries,
but some are original—such as WESOM (We Saved Our
Marriage). Brennan features two themes that help account
for the church's power and outreach in lay ministries:
(1) "*Need* is a key word. . . . We are a church that seeks to
discover people's needs they don't even know that they
have." (2) "Small communities are absolutely crucial so
that people are involved in faith-sharing spirituality rather
than the kind of mindless volunteerism that marks too
much of what we think of as 'successful' churches."[21]

The Indispensable Role of Small Groups

Brennan's last comment represents the four best-kept
secrets about large growing churches—Catholic, Protestant,
or Pentecostal—and all four secrets relate to small groups.

1. Churches grow larger by growing smaller. That is, as
   the church multiplies small groups and other small
   faith-sharing communities, and as it involves more
   and more of its people in small groups, and as it
   involves seekers in small groups before they ever

believe or commit, and as its increasing numbers of small groups are reaching out to more and more pre-Christian people, those dynamics substantially contribute to the growth of the church.

2. Small group experience develops people for ministry. The genius of the small group *koinonia* is that people minister to one another within the small group experience. As we support one another, pull for one another, hold one another accountable, rejoice with one another, weep with one another, and intercede for one another, the Holy Spirit helps us become "members of one another" (Eph. 4:25). Some of our deepest needs are met in the small group, or they, likely, are not met at all.

3. The small group functions as a laboratory of lay ministry, a setting in which we observe lay ministry being modeled over and over, in which we learn approaches to caring ministry from one another, and in which we make our first attempts at ministering to someone else. Most of the people who engage in a lay ministry learned how in a small group, and a small group still supports them in their lay ministry.

4. The small group also functions as a laboratory for the witness of the laity. Each week, in the small group, people talk about the gospel, what Jesus Christ means to them, and what the Holy Spirit is doing in their lives. Each week, they hear one another share on the same matters, and they learn more and better ways to communicate these matters, meaningfully, from one another. They consult with one another about people they are now attempting to reach. They "lift up" one another for the life of outreach and invitation. The experience "lubricates the tongue." People who regularly talk about the gospel in a group are more likely to talk about the gospel outside the group, and to people outside the household of faith.

In all of the apostolic movements we have studied, people are reached, supported, developed in, and deployed from, small groups. Celtic Christianity prepared people in small groups at the monastic communities, reached out through apostolic teams to tribal settlements, and (judging from their very small chapels) raised up local churches composed of many intimate fellowships.[22] Eighteenth century Methodism reached and ministered to people through distinctive lay-led groups called "classes"; Methodism then developed more disciplined disciples through the small groups called "bands."[23] The Pentecostal movement has grown, almost everywhere, through the proliferation of small groups of people who minister to one another and reach seekers. The movement's showcase church is the Central Full Gospel Church of Seoul, Korea, which, through the outreach of more than 25,000 lay-led "home cell groups," has grown to more than 740,000 members![24]

For reasons like these, Bruce Larson declares "it is just as important that you be involved in a small group as it is to believe that Jesus Christ died for your sins. There are many things that God can only do for you, and through you, through the contagious life of the small group." For reasons like these, Ralph Neighbor contends that it is no accident, or random occurrence, that 19 of the 20 largest churches on earth are "cell churches." For reasons like these, many church leaders observe that, worldwide and long-term, wherever the clergy are expected to do most of the ministry, the church stagnates or declines; wherever the laity do most of the ministry, with the clergy "leading and feeding" the laity for their mission, the church thrives and grows.[25]

The previous chapter contended that Christianity must be presented in "culturally relevant" ways to become contagious among a people. This chapter has featured apostolic ministry as a lay movement, shaped and empowered through small group formation. One twentieth-century case may dramatize the three themes of cultural relevance, small groups, and lay ministries more than any other.

Christianity first established a presence in China in the seventh century and a continuing presence for the last several centuries, but growth was slow. Christianity's ranks had grown to only about four million Christians when Communism gained control, and Chairman Mao imposed the "Cultural Revolution" in 1949. One of Mao's objectives was to "cleanse" China of all "foreign influences," including "foreign religions," which included Christianity. All foreign missionaries were sent home, Chinese clergy were defrocked, church buildings were "secularized." In the West, we heard very little from Chinese believers; we usually assumed that Mao's project must be succeeding, that the Church in China was decimated. Although the persecution of China's Christians continues to this day, the Cultural Revolution per se ended in 1969, and we gradually discovered what had really been happening those twenty years. The Christian faith had *not* been eliminated; indeed, its ranks had grown from about four million to about forty million. The growth of Chinese Christianity has continued; by 2000, the numbers of Christians in China exceeded seventy million.

What accounts for the remarkable growth of the Church in such intimidating circumstances? The growth can be substantially accounted for, in human terms, by three factors. The Church was driven underground, where (1) the faith assumed a "more Chinese face." With missionaries gone and clergy defrocked, Chinese Christianity (2) became a lay movement; all of the ministry that matters was now done by laypeople. Lay leaders (3) reinvented the "house church"; small groups meeting in homes, usually in secret and often at great risk, multiplied across much of the land.

These three strategic factors, alone, cannot fully account for China's apostolic explosion; the Christians often knew that the Lord was with them, in providence and power. Nevertheless, the policy of "the Lord of the Harvest" is to reach people through us, and the culturally indigenous lay movement appears to be his universal instrument of choice, everywhere.

CHAPTER FIVE

Recovery Ministries As a Prototype for Outreach Ministries

When my wife and I gathered with other worshipers at St. Luke United Methodist Church in Lexington, Kentucky, on Easter Sunday, 2002, I had no idea that the two testimonies to be featured in that service would dramatize the future of Christianity's mission in North America.

Dawn Wallin, a housewife and mother of three young girls, was celebrating her first Easter as a Christian. Dawn had attended a Sunday school several times as a girl, and later her wedding was in a church; but essentially she had no Christian background, and she sometimes wondered, "What is that fish on the back of some cars?" A problem with anger had been consuming her and was now causing other problems in her life. Her girls started attending Sunday school at St. Luke, and, just seven months before she spoke for our Easter service, she and her husband, Eric, attended worship for the first time. "I have to admit the very first sermon I heard from Pastor Steve [Martyn] spoke to me (and every one since), so we kept coming."

Several women invited Dawn to a Wednesday morning Bible study; she jumped at the chance to get out of the house and do something for herself in the company of other women. "So there I was, walking into a study on the book of John, never having read the Bible before!" As she got to know the women, she recalls wanting what they had—something she could not quite name. One Wednesday morning, the group studied the John 5 story, in which, beside the healing pool at Bethesda, Jesus asks a lame man, "Do you want to get well? If you do, get up and walk!"

> I must have read these verses thirty times. I burst into tears because I knew that was me—that thirty-something person with this enormous load to bear, so heavy and consuming I couldn't move. No, it wasn't a physical ailment, but it was preventing me from moving forward in my life. And there Jesus was, asking me, "Do you want to get well?" He had the cure; I just had to be obedient and follow. I remember uttering "yes," and at that moment Jesus leapt off that page and into my heart. He said what no one else could say, "You are fixable and I forgive you. Now get up and walk!"

Weeks later, when the group was studying the story of the death of Lazarus in John 11, Dawn was struck by verse 35: "Jesus wept." She inferred that "he was weeping because Mary was weeping. He feels that ache that we all feel when someone we love is sad." Dawn then realized, "He knows my heart. He understands me. So I started to pray about everyday things." Our congregation could sense, with Dawn, that she was only at "the beginning of an amazing journey. . . . So I stand before you as a work in progress. Thank you for helping me find my home."

Then Gordon Henson, in his midforties, stood to reflect on the "career" that consumed him from ages fifteen to forty. The career he spoke of, metaphorically, was alcoholism. Drinking became the priority, then the obsession, of his existence. "On the way home every day would be a stop by the bar for a couple of doubles, followed by a couple of beers with shots, before stopping by the liquor store for more of the same. I thought I was in control of my drinking, but denial had taken over." His addiction, in time, cost him the completion of his college education, several jobs, and two marriages. In the wake of his second failed marriage, he reported, "I hit my bottom. I was beaten. Alcohol had won." In this season of his life, he reported, "The scales from my eyes began to fall away and the fog of denial began to lift. I could begin to see the destruction left from my alcoholic wake."

Then, Gordon told us,

> The Lord used a lot of men in this town who loved me when I didn't know how to love myself. Through them and with the support of family and good friends, I began the road to recovery and discovery. I began to see and feel the power, grace, and love of God upon me. I began each morning, and continue to do so, with Scripture reading and prayer, asking for strength, courage, and the desire not to drink this day. Each one of my days ends with praise for not drinking, looking to see where I may have wronged or hurt others, and the direction to set it right. I now have a relationship with God through Jesus Christ—something I didn't know was possible in my younger days.

Several years into sobriety, Gordon can still experience the fears, frustrations, and cravings that were once destroying him; but God, the recovery community, and St. Luke Church combine to keep him on the safe side. Furthermore, he reported, "I continue with God's help and strength to clear away the wreckage of my past. . . . So I continue to press on, to grow to be more like Jesus as Jesus is more in me."

In response to Dawn's and Gordon's testimonies, the congregation stood to applaud, and then cheered; there were few dry eyes in the sanctuary. On that Easter Sunday, in church of all places, we knew that, for that moment, we were all close to the power that raised Jesus from death.

Dawn and Gordon represent the future of Christian outreach in the West. We are called, in the apostolic tradition, to the radical outreach that engages people like Dawn—"secular" people who do not even know what we Christians are talking about, with no Christian memory and no church to "return to."[1] Furthermore, we are called, in the apostolic tradition, to the even more radical outreach that engages people like Gordon who most "establishment people" gave up on long ago. Because, as we experienced in church that Sunday at St. Luke, when the "regular" people experience someone they'd have once viewed as "hopeless" now greatly changed, they become more open to the gospel's power.

Gordon's case is also useful because, for several years, I have asked church leaders to identify the types of people who their church members would believe to be the hardest people to reach. Their people, they say, would regard addicts to alcohol or some other drug as very difficult to reach. Indeed, many "good church people" perceive addicted people as so "bad," "hijacked," or "out of control" that they cannot imagine them liberated and in their "right mind." Their perception is often rooted in an extended-family experience; many people have watched a relative, say, drink himself into a kind of madness and an early grave, and the family will never forget how powerless they felt. In *The Celtic Way of Evangelism*, I suggest that "people with addictions are among the most obvious, and least understood, New Barbarians in the West today."[2]

Addiction, As (Mis)understood, in Historical Perspective

Most churches, essentially, write off the huge addicted population. Estimates of the addicted population's size can vary. A Hazelden Institute report suggests that "the prevalence of substance abuse disorders in the general population is about 16%."[3] Another report suggests that as many as "a quarter of the U.S. population is hooked on alcohol, cocaine, amphetamines or some other substance."[4] The problem of addicted people is compounded by the fact that they are likely to be unchurched; so, typically, they have no community of faith to dissuade them from experimenting or using, they now have no community of faith to help them recover, and they feel that no church would really want to take a chance on them. They usually feel "stigmatized" by church people. So the people who often need God the most are the least likely to come to church.

The church, like most of society, has long assumed that bad character, weak willpower, and/or irresponsible parents are the sole known causes of addiction. Many church people react emotionally toward addicted people the way the ancient Jews did toward lepers. Ken Chafin once addressed a gathering of Baptist men on the importance of relational support in tough times. He posed a hypothetical question: "You have just been informed that your son has been arrested and charged with possession of drugs. Who would you want to know?" Chafin meant it as a rhetorical question, but one man spoke up: "I'll tell you who I would *not* want to know. The people at church." Chafin observed heads nodding in agreement throughout the auditorium.

The literature on addiction, chemical dependency, and recovery is filled with definitions of addiction. Each definition features part of the problem; together, they are in substantial agreement.

- Addiction is not a choice, but a sickness or a disease— not a disease like measles or polio, but a sickness that some people are biologically vulnerable to, such as an allergy, diabetes, or (more recently) schizophrenia or bipolar disorder.[5]
- Craving (or compulsion or obsession) increasingly overrides the addict's willpower, changes the way the addict thinks, and drives his or her addicted behavior.
- Addiction is a progressive disease. So, at some point, a person cannot control drug use, particularly while using, and his or her life becomes out of control.
- In time, the person is powerless to quit using, even if aware of the impact and the consequences; the addiction now adversely affects every area of a person's life and has changed the person profoundly.

So the line from Lou Reed's song "Heroin" is very revealing: "Heroin, it's my wife and it's my life." Several lines from "My Name Is Cocaine," by a local anonymous inmate in a Lexington, Kentucky, prison, suggest the drug's power to co-opt anyone's life:

> *I'll make a schoolboy forget his books;*
> *I'll make a beauty queen forget her looks;*
> *I'll take a renowned speaker and make him a bore;*
> *I'll take your mama and make her a whore.*

I have found Bill White's shorthand definition of addiction very useful: "Compulsive use in spite of adverse consequences." Alcoholics Anonymous meetings usually begin by quoting the famous lines from chapter 5 of the "big book": "Remember that we deal with alcohol—cunning, baffling, powerful! Without help it is too much for us.

But there is One who has all power—that One is God. May you find Him now!"[6]

The Multiple (Known) Causes of Addiction[7]

We are reasonably clear today of at least five causes of addiction, and these causes seem to operate in combination.

First, an informed consensus recognizes that some people have a much greater "genetic vulnerability" to alcoholism (and presumably to similar substance addictions) than others. Early studies observed a correlation between parents and children; compared to the population as a whole, a person is twice as likely to be addicted if one parent was addicted and four times as likely if both parents were addicted. Early studies likewise observed a strong positive correlation in identical twins—whether reared together in the homes of the biological parents or reared in separate adoptive homes.

Several genes are implicated in the development of addiction. One of these genes is named DRD2—the "pleasure-seeking gene."

> UCLA studies of brain tissue showed that individuals with the "A1 variation" of the DRD2 gene have specifically fewer dopamine receptors in pleasure centers of the brain. The findings suggest that many addicts use drugs, which increase brain dopamine levels, to compensate for the deficiency in their neurological pleasure system. . . . It means that people with this genetic trait are much more susceptible to addiction.[8]

In the general population, 10 percent have the A1 variation of this gene; in the addicted population, 50 percent have the A1 variation. Variations in at least several other genes are known to make people more vulnerable, and variations in

125

many more genes are suspected. Across a population, the actual difference in vulnerability between "addicts" and "normal people" is only one of degree; most people may be vulnerable to some degree. (Many "normal people," following surgery, have experienced addiction to a prescription drug; many others get hooked on tranquilizers.)

Second, the drugs themselves have addictive powers. Some drugs are more addictive than others; $50 worth of a certain strain of cocaine can hook a majority of people for life. Some drugs are increasing in their power to induce addiction; through underground scientific horticulture, much of the marijuana on the streets today has more than ten times the addictive power of the marijuana of the 1960s. Most drugs act on the brain's "pleasure center" and boost the dopamine action that induces the feelings of pleasure. In time, the nerve cells (by themselves) trigger less dopamine, and the brain is then more dependent upon drugs for pleasure. This is the source of the craving that hijacks the addict's willpower and life. Because of this craving, "Willpower alone is helpless in the face of addiction. . . . The brain of a drug user . . . is physically altered in ways that make it difficult to resist further use."[9] The addictive person's brain is thus primed for relapse.

Third, psychological factors may play a role in addiction.[10] Folk wisdom within the recovery movement claims that sensitive and deeply emotional people are more easily and more deeply hurt and are more likely to avail of the drug's synthetic consolation. Perfectionist personalities, who fail to attain their excessive expectations, are more likely to self-medicate the feelings they attach to failure. People who expect, to an unrealistic degree, life to bring them beauty and happiness often escape from reality into a chemically induced experience of beauty. In a scene from the Jack Lemmon film *Days of Wine and Roses*, a fellow has found recovery in Alcoholics Anonymous. His girlfriend drops by his apartment and invites him to rejoin her in the bar scene, but he encourages her to join him in the life of recovery. As she stands and looks out the high-rise apartment window on New York City, she responds after lengthy thought: "I can't, I can't, I can't! When I look out this window sober it's cheap, and it's dirty, and it's ugly; but when I look out drunk, it's beautiful."

By the time a person enters even the early middle stages of the addictive process, other psychological factors—called defense mechanisms—kick in, shield and reinforce the disease, and militate against recovery. The most widely observed defense games that addicts play include denial (or minimizing), rationalizing, illusion of control, memory distortion, and truth distortion—but especially denial. As the recovery community often jokes, "Denial is not just a river in Egypt!"

Fourth, there are "systemic" factors behind the addiction epidemic. Much of the Western media's music, television, and movies serve to glamorize, and legitimize, the use and abuse of drugs. Furthermore, as the Michael Douglas film *Traffic* dramatized, the world's formidable "cartels" cultivate drugs, and organize their distribution, with superior technology, and ruthless power, for enormous profit.

Fifth, profound cultural factors are also at work in addiction and in recovery. Bill White's penetrating analysis in *Pathways from the Culture of Addiction to the Culture of Recovery* is indispensable in elaborating this essential insight.[11] White describes the process in which the "culture of addiction" draws a vulnerable person into a "tribe," or a "social world," that introduces, reinforces, and celebrates drug abuse and resocializes the person into a different identity. For instance, initiates acquire a new *language* and conversation themes, while losing the capacity to talk about their feelings. They enter a new world of *symbols*—paraphernalia, logos, specific clothing or jewelry, and "articles associated with hustling behavior such as beepers." Addiction becomes involved with *institutions*—places such as saloons in the old West associated with abuse—and with daily *rituals* that trigger abuse—such as after meals or between activities—or with more elaborate rituals (such as a needle-sharing ritual). The culture of addiction develops or uses *music*, such as the music that legitimizes rage and glorifies cocaine use, reaching repetitively into the addict's right brain to confirm the culture's beliefs and values, to make the drug lifestyle seem "normal," and to trigger craving. The new recruit internalizes a local tribal *history*, which is

> passed on through stories and folktales. Most of these stories, which serve as a primary vehicle to transmit values, revolve around significant tribal events and personalities. "Hustling tales" become a way of transmitting knowledge and techniques to neophytes about various cons. Descriptions of heroes depicted in these tales become a way of shaping desired personality attributes of cultural members. "Copping tales" are used to teach neophytes the skills and dangers [involved] in procuring drugs. "Getting-off tales" convey a whole body of folklore and folk medicine on how to use and reduce risks associated with use. "Enemy tales" reinforce cultural paranoia and teach neophytes how to cope with cultural enemies, e.g., undercover agents, snitches, nonsmokers, supervisors, dealers who peddle "garbage," "shrinks," and "crazies."[12]

White describes twenty *roles* that various tribal members live out as they support and expand the culture of addiction. The "dealer," for example, provides drugs of choice for the members. The "high priest" champions the culture's values and drug use and targets possible new converts. The "storyteller" is the culture's oral historian. The "medicine man" has folk remedies for hangovers, overdoses, and infections. The "jailhouse lawyer" helps members cope with law enforcement agencies and treatment professionals. Other roles, such as the "hustler," the "ambassador," the celebrity addict, the "crazies," and the "profiteers," expose the remarkably sophisticated culture that sustains and bolsters the addictive lifestyle.

In time, White reports, involvement with the drug and the drug culture changes a person's identity and religious orientation. Before drug use, some persons were religious, some ignored religion, and some were emotionally rejecting their religious roots; such differences disappear as addiction takes over. Addiction, however, makes neither atheists nor agnostics.

> Addiction, until the latest stages, renders questions of God and religion insignificant. Addiction is so consuming there simply is no energy available to raise religious questions, let alone ponder answers. Addiction becomes one's religion, drugs become one's God, and rituals of use become rites of worship.[13]

We can add that the local tribe of addiction becomes the addict's surrogate church; and the drug-induced "high" functions as a counterfeit religious experience, in which the person *feels* justified and at one with Reality. In time, the experience and the community combine to instill new values, a new morality, and a new lifestyle; and the convert is substantially changed into the drug culture's image. All addicts who enter recovery, however, become clear that the drug-induced "religious experiences" were delusional, and the addictive community's "religion" was deeply destructive.[14]

In fact, the total drug experience is so social, consuming, and transformative, that liberating addicts from their "friends" in the culture of addiction is often more difficult than liberating them from the drug. For this reason, membership and involvement in a "culture of recovery" is necessary for a person's liberation from the twin powers of the drug and the drug culture. I will be suggesting that churches are uniquely positioned, in every city, to provide the needed groups, communities, and meetings for people in recovery, and that the church is called to be the local recovery movement's greatest ally.

Addiction and Recovery in Informed Perspective

So addiction is much less caused by "choice" and "character" than the churches have usually assumed; whereas personality and the drug's addictive power play greater roles than the churches have known, and genetic and cultural forces play enormously greater causal roles than most church leaders have ever guessed. Granted, the typical addict did exercise some choice in ingesting the first drink, puff, or injection. Though some petty adolescent rebellion may stand behind "the first time," many people ingest for the first time by accident as they navigate in social circles, in which party usage is normal; in most cases, forces such as curiosity, joining in socially, or peer influence are usually much stronger than "conscious sin."

The first time often occurs in a period during which people feel invincible, even if they have observed other people hooked or craving; "It couldn't happen to me!" Neither the drug nor the people of the drug culture ever honestly present the first "fix" as something that could destroy you; it promises pleasure and friends, insight and religious experience. Once the brain chemistry changes and the craving begins, however, willpower plays an ever-diminishing role. In any case, no one chooses to become addicted; in that sense, at least, addiction is a no-fault disease. Doug Toft of the Hazelden Foundation elaborates:

> No one raises a glass of alcohol, snorts a line of cocaine, or lights up a nicotine-laden cigarette with a toast: "Here's to addiction." When first using these drugs, people simply choose to do something that makes them feel good. But with continued use, these people can find themselves addicted. They depend on the drug not simply to feel good

but to feel *normal*. Using drugs is no longer a choice but a compulsion. These people don't plan to become addicts; it just happens.[15]

Addiction is a "progressive" disease; it gets worse over time. There are almost as many classifications of the disease's "stages" as there are writers, but a typical sequence moves from a period of initial use, to "issues" around use, to abuse, to compulsive use, to chemical dependence. There is some consensus about the indicators that a person is in a compulsive or dependence stage. The person

- has an increased tolerance for the drug, so he or she has to ingest more this week to achieve the "high" experienced last week
- sometimes engages in spontaneous unplanned use
- after the first drink, cannot stop drinking
- begins using alone
- goes on binges
- becomes increasingly preoccupied with the drug and the local drug tribe
- plans more intentionally and elaborately for acquiring and using the drug
- begins to hoard and protect his supply
- uses the drug to self-medicate depression or feelings of low self-esteem.

Addiction is a "complete" disease, in the sense that, in time, it affects and changes the complete person. John MacDougall of the Hazelden Foundation observes that the drug activates the addiction to attack us spiritually first; then the addictive process typically moves from spiritual, to emotional, to mental, and finally to one's physical health.[16] One's continuing ability to function mentally can, for a while, fuel the denial that is addiction's chief defense mechanism. Even when mental performance deteriorates, the addict's body can remain strong for a while.

The case of Dave Draper is well known in some circles. A physique champion in the 1960s, Dave was named Mr. America, Mr. World, and Mr. Universe. He acted in Hollywood movies and joined the Hollywood party culture—including its booze and drug culture. He became addicted and, in time, lost his high-living livelihood and everything else. He recalls: "I saw my family depart and my sinister, cynical companions, drugs and alcohol, lead me from my home to a barren gardener's shed in a little orchard on the edge of Nowhere. No power, no running water, no bucks, no buddy. Hey, I still had the weights, was still lifting, never stopped."[17]

Recovery, John MacDougall tells us, typically proceeds in the *opposite* order: One begins physical recovery first, as in the several days of "detox." After two weeks or more, a person starts moving out of "stinkin' thinkin' " and into more normal thinking.[18] One's emotional health begins returning still later. A spiritual awakening typically comes last.[19] In 1983, Dave Draper nearly died from congestive heart failure. He entered recovery and, in time, experienced restored health, better thinking, healthier emotions, and the gift of faith and new life. Today, he openly professes Jesus Christ as Lord and is deeply involved in a church in Santa Cruz, California, that serves as a "recovery community" for Dave and many other people. He has remarried, he owns and manages the World Gym in Santa Cruz, and, now approaching sixty, Dave still pumps iron.

The Story, the Steps, and the Serenity Prayer

While some Christian traditions, particularly the Salvation Army, were in ministry with addicted people long before an organized recovery movement, the movement began with the founding of Alcoholics Anonymous in 1935.[20] Bill Wilson, an attorney in New York City, was treated for alcoholism several times and relapsed after each treatment. Facing the possibility of permanent commitment to an institution, he connected with Dr. William Silkworth—who convinced him that his affliction was rooted in a disease more than in moral failure or lack of willpower—and he connected with the Rev. Samuel Shoemaker and Calvary Episcopal Church in New York City. He experienced a Christian awakening and a commitment to helping other alcoholics; but he still experienced the "craving," episodically.

One night, while Wilson was on a trip to Akron, Ohio, the craving returned. He acted on the plan that, when he experienced craving, he would find and help another alcoholic. The man he found was a physician, Robert Smith, who became the movement's famous "Dr. Bob."[21] They found a third man, and that moment is recognized as the founding of the Alcoholics Anonymous movement. The leaders knew, early, that the movement had to function independently of the organized denominations; many church people were judgmental toward addicted people, and, fearing judgment, most addicts would not go to churches.

From that modest beginning, Alcoholics Anonymous is thought to have over 2 million active members in the U.S.A. and Canada, with a presence in 171 countries.[22] AA's expanding influence is reflected in the sales of the "big book." More than 300,000 copies of the first edition (1939) of *Alcoholics Anonymous* were published, more than 1,150,500 copies of the second edition (1955), and more than 11,698,000 of the third edition (1976). Its famous "Twelve Step" approach to recovery has spawned organizations for people gripped by other addictions—organizations such as Narcotics Anonymous, Gamblers Anonymous, Overeaters Anonymous, Sex Addicts Anonymous, and organizations for friends and relatives of addicts, such as Al-Anon, Alateen, and GamAnon; each follows an adapted version of the Twelve Steps.

So the greatest legacy of early AA to all people needing recovery (from any substance or process) is the Twelve Steps. With Sam Shoemaker as facilitator, Bill Wilson and Dr. Bob reflected upon their recovery experience and upon relevant passages in the New Testament—especially the book of James, the Sermon on the Mount, and chapter 13 of 1 Corinthians.[23] The clarification process went through several drafts; at one early point, they had clarified six steps. The following Twelve Steps have stood the tests of extensive time and scrutiny.

1. We admitted we were powerless over alcohol—that our lives had become unmanageable.
2. Came to believe that a Power greater than ourselves could restore us to sanity.
3. Made a decision to turn our will and our lives over to the care of God *as we understood Him.*
4. Made a searching and fearless moral inventory of ourselves.
5. Admitted to God, to ourselves, and to another human being the exact nature of our wrongs.
6. Were entirely ready to have God remove all these defects of character.
7. Humbly asked Him to remove our shortcomings.
8. Made a list of all persons we had harmed, and became willing to make amends to them all.
9. Made direct amends to such people wherever possible, except when to do so would injure them or others.
10. Continued to take personal inventory and when we were wrong promptly admitted it.
11. Sought through prayer and meditation to improve our conscious contact with God *as we understood Him,* praying only for knowledge of His will for us and the power to carry that out.
12. Having had a spiritual awakening as the result of these steps, we tried to carry this message to alco-

holics, and to practice these principles in all our affairs.[24]

A careful reading of the Twelve Steps reveals that steps one through five constitute the heart of the process. Steps six through eleven engage in the kind of go-deeper redundancy and specificity that experience revealed to be necessary for healthy lifelong recovery. Step twelve makes the process available to other addicts, though—as Bill Wilson discovered from the movement's beginning—living out the twelfth step is a necessary part of one's own recovery. My colleague Dr. George Ross characterizes four stages in recovery: (1) giving up (steps one through three), (2) owning up (steps four through seven) (3) making up (steps eights and nine), and (4) growing up (steps ten through twelve).

The "big book" is still able to report that "rarely have we seen a person fail who has thoroughly followed our path."[25] A leader reads the Twelve Steps in every AA meeting; people in recovery rehearse the Twelve Steps for the rest of their lives. Meetings often feature the testimonies of one or more persons. Meetings usually close as the people pray the Lord's Prayer.

The other liturgical component prominent in AA meetings is the Serenity Prayer from the pen of Reinhold Niebuhr. They usually pray only the first part, but the whole prayer features essential perspective and wisdom:

God, grant me
The serenity to accept the things I cannot change;
The courage to change the things I can;
The wisdom to know the difference.

Living one day at a time;
Enjoying one moment at a time;
Accepting hardship as

the pathway to peace.
Taking, as He did, this sinful world
as it is, not as I would have it;
Trusting that He will make all things
right if I surrender to His will;
That I may be reasonably happy in
this life, and supremely happy
with Him forever in the Next.

The establishment of the Hazelden Foundation is probably the other pivotal event in the history of the recovery movement. In 1947, leaders from two treatment centers in the Minneapolis area met at a farmhouse, with concern for reaching alcoholics before they "hit bottom" and lose everything.[26] They opened the first of their recovery institutions in 1949 and gradually developed a twenty-eight-day process that begins with "detox" and then combines the strengths of medical, psychological, and spiritual approaches, with the power of group support, to help a person get through the first five steps within the twenty-eight-day period.

What became known as "the Minnesota Model" of recovery builds upon AA and the Twelve Steps and is predicated on two revolutionary principles: First, the Hazelden Foundation learned that an alcoholic's initial motivation for getting into treatment, even if it is to pacify his or her family, is *not* especially a predictor of treatment outcome; the recovery rate is about as good for people who did not want to come as for people who did want to come. Second, Hazelden's compassionate ethic mandates that addicts always be treated "with dignity and respect." Over the years, Hazelden has engaged in extensive research and experimentation and, today, publishes about one half of the earth's recovery literature published.

Addiction and Recovery in Theological Perspective

Some church leaders express anxiety about the recovery movement's less-than-adequate understanding of God, its frequent use of the term "Higher Power," and its references to "God as we understand Him."

AA and its spin-off movements, admittedly, have a limited focus. They limit their mission to the immense challenge of helping addicts achieve sobriety and regain sanity. (Christianity, of course, is about that and much more.) Consequently, AA emphasizes God's role in the miracle of recovery; so, from recovery literature, one is unlikely to arrive, say, at an adequate understanding of the Trinity or the Incarnation or the Christian life or social ethic.

Yet AA has recovered some elements of Christianity and the faithful life that the mainline churches have virtually ignored. For instance, how many regular pew sitters would even consider the invitation to "make a searching and fearless moral inventory" or admit to God and to another human being "the exact nature of our wrongs" or are "entirely ready to have God remove all these defects of character," or genuinely seek "the will of God" for their lives? How many churches are as confident as AA is that God is present and available to rescue people from very deep weeds and to change lives profoundly?

AA is essentially a lay movement; how many churches are as confident as AA is that God can do great things for the people in deep weeds through laity? Many people in AA are clear that involvement in the twelfth step—carrying the message to other alcoholics—is essential to their own recovery; how many Christians know that outreach is important in their own redemption? Compared to AA meetings, how many church services can you attend and know that miracles are sitting all around you?

The fact that AA sometimes refers to "God" and sometimes to a "Higher Power" is easily defended. The biblical writers employ many names for God, and the World Church refers to God with an astonishing range of indigenous names.[27] The three letter symbol G-O-D is only one of many Germanic names for the deity; the fairly wide diffusion of the name was largely accidental. In recent history, the interest in avoiding "sexist" terms has influenced some people away from names such as "Father"; but there are no compelling reasons to use one name only, and many reasons to use many names!

The idea that we begin with God "as we understand Him" is also easily defended. This nuance was pioneered in Sam Shoemaker's ministry of evangelism, in which he invited people "to bring as much of yourself as you understand to as much of God as you understand," and God will take you from there. What was Shoemaker's justification for this approach? That is how God begins with everyone! It is the only way we can begin our pilgrimage with God. Although I am an orthodox theologian, I have been forced to observe the degree to which our Lord is "relaxed" about people getting all the theology straight before they can begin a new life with him. John MacDougall suggests that struggling people may need to believe only three things to begin with God: (1) God is not me, (2) God is greater than me, and (3) God is willing to help me.

Some church leaders get upset when they hear recovery movement people (and *many* other people) say that "spirituality" is desirable, but one does not have to be "religious." It is important to understand what they mean, and what they are affirming, by the distinction between "spiritual" and "religious." "Spirituality," as they see it, is based on experience and consists of the quality of the relationships between the self and nature, other people, and the Higher Power; "religion," as they see it, consists of dogmas, moral codes, traditions, and ecclesiastical and institutional concerns. With the twin caveats that Christianity has been entrusted with Truth to share and an Ethic to shape us, we should affirm their point. True Christianity is more about good news for new relationships than what they perceive it basically to be about.

The tangling of issues such as addiction, responsibility, sin, and evil produces the most confusion; but it is possible to state several insights clearly.[28] I believe that AA and Hazelden are substantially right: Although some choice is involved in the first experiment, other forces (such as curiosity, peer pressure, and assumed invincibility) are present, and, in any case, no one chooses to become an addict; in that sense, addiction is a no-fault disease. Human weakness is undoubtedly involved; and the drug, the drug culture, and transcendent Evil all exploit people's weaknesses. The more one is hooked and chemically dependent, the less free one's will becomes.

The drug and the drug culture make a greater sinner of anyone who gets hijacked. Bill White tells us that

addiction is not just a disease of the body; . . . [it] is also a disease of values. Addicts regularly violate, through addiction-related behavior, values they still claim to hold. . . . Addicts . . . become somebody different when they use. . . . The intoxication-induced personality will commit acts that would be unthinkable to the nonusing personality.[29]

This is perhaps the worst-kept secret about addiction. Under the influence of the drug, or the craving for the drug, people deceive, lie, cheat, steal, and engage in a range of immoral behaviors that cause the shame that then oppresses them. Moreover, the protracted drug experience changes people at the core; they become astonishingly self-centered and narcissistic. When I took the Hazelden Foundation's seminar for pastors, I spent time daily with the men of the Shoemaker residential unit. One fellow, who'd been a heroic outdoorsman and deep-sea diver before his "crash," came in from an afternoon in the garden. He approached me to report this experience: "George,

I just discovered something important, really important. I was out there lying on a blanket, feeling the wind and looking up at birds, and butterflies, and clouds for over an hour. Suddenly, I knew, I knew that it's not all about me. The universe is not all about me!" I knew that salvation had moved nearer to him.

We have a "legion" of reasons to believe that Evil plays a major role in addiction. Art Glasser, once dean of the School of World Mission at Fuller Theological Seminary, use to observe "The form that possessive and destructive Evil takes varies from one age to another, from one culture to another. Its most characteristic form in our culture, in our time, is addiction." In addiction, something like possession by a supra-mundane force, hostile to our health and happiness, but pretending to be our friend and lover, is involved. Indeed, the first of the Twelve Steps involves the acknowledgment that we are in the grips of something bigger than us, from which we cannot free ourselves. Addiction, however, is not precisely like ancient demonic possession, because recovery usually involves a lifelong process more than a "casting out" at one point in time. We know that Evil is also involved in a more comprehensive way: The network of people and organizations who cultivate, transport, distribute, promote, glamorize, and push drugs are conspirators in a destructive Evil greater than the network of global terrorism.

The issue of responsibility remains. We know that the addict is less responsible for becoming an addict than we once thought; but once the denial is penetrated, and detox and early recovery are history, the addict is responsible for doing the things necessary to stay in active recovery. Family and friends are responsible for abandoning their denial and codependency, for insisting that the addict get into treatment, and, later, for supporting the person in recovery.

Furthermore, the churches are responsible to support (to

provide, if necessary) the local "culture of recovery" in every community. Churches are responsible for ministries to, and with, people in recovery and for helping addicts begin recovery. Churches are *not* responsible for attempting what churches cannot do; most addicts must experience detox and time in an intensive recovery institution before churches and local recovery movements can be effective for their ongoing recovery. Even fully staffed halfway houses cannot help people before they have experienced detox and the early stages of recovery; neither can churches.

Opportunities in Recovery Ministries

AA's Twelfth Step is critically important because it matters whether addictive people have the opportunity to be liberated from the delusions and powers that are destroying them. Indeed, the church's mandate—to give all people the live option of opening their lives to the Higher Power revealed in Jesus Christ—is more critically important than most churches have owned. Local churches face a great opportunity to serve and reach a vast population that, historically, most churches have ignored. This opportunity can be expressed in many specific possibilities.

For instance, a local church can provide rooms and hospitality for a range of Twelve Step recovery groups. Or the church can offer recovery groups as an expression of the church's ministry. Saddleback Church, in Orange County, California, devotes Friday evenings to people in recovery. Following a meal and a worship service with a speaker addressing some recovery issue or theme, people meet in one of many specific groups—including groups for chemically dependent men and women, for codependent men and women, for people with sexual addictions, and for people in relationships with those who have a sexual addiction, and distinct groups focusing on anger, eating disorders, financial recovery, relationship addiction, and abused women. Saddleback's "Celebrate Recovery" materials are now published and are used in the recovery ministries of many other churches.[30]

Local churches are called to include recovering people in their ranks, in ways that build on, supplement, and complete, the AA experience; there is, after all, a fuller revelation of God than is found in the Serenity Prayer, and there is more to the Abundant Life than sobriety and sanity. A church can become a church that understands addiction and addicted people and wants and welcomes them. The church can teach its people about the causes and nature of addiction and the way of recovery. The church can engage in social advocacy and political lobbying for addicted people who still experience misunderstanding and discrimination in the wider community. The church that is expanding its range of "alternative worship services" can offer, say, a 12:30 P.M. Sunday service for people in recovery and their families, and the pastor can offer "Fifth Step ministry" (addicts admitting to other human beings the exact nature of their wrongs) when people reach that stage in their recovery. The church can offer educational, group, and counseling ministries for and with families of addicted people. The church can, and must, deploy its own Christians-in-recovery in ministries to other people in recovery. God has prepared them, through the addiction and recovery experience, to be in ministry with their peers; besides, many addicts will only trust another addict.

Local churches are also called to recognize, whether their denomination permits or prohibits drinking, that the addiction epidemic has *not* bypassed their membership; virtually every church has some members and attendees who abuse alcohol and drugs. John MacDougall reports that the Hazelden Foundation's twenty-eight-day residential recovery program receives many "empty shell alcoholics and addicts"; they are still nice people and still attend church and think of themselves as Christians, but they "have massive drinking or drug problems which have not yet produced the stunning wreckage" that addiction produces in time. "Their exterior still looks good: home, church, family, friends, golf club membership, but inside they are dying," and "the addiction that has hollowed out their family life has hollowed out any genuine Christianity they might have had." These people, MacDougall submits, "need God just as much as the 'barbarian' alcoholics." So the typical local church is called to abandon its denial and codependency; a church is *not* obligated to protect the most pathological secrets of its members. A church is called to care enough and dare enough to hold people accountable, to join their families in insisting that they get help, and to provide ministries for Christians in recovery.[31]

Moreover, churches are called to serve as allies, and influencers, of AA and the other recovery movements. "Secularization" has influenced the recovery community to some extent (though perhaps not as much as it has influenced the mainline denominations), so some groups are not as close to Christianity as early AA was, and some groups tend to neglect the Twelfth Step. Those groups are not reaching as many people as the more "orthodox" and "evangelical" groups, and, I am told, the relapse rate of the people they involve is higher.

Recovery ministries are also important because they serve as a prototype for many other outreach ministries. At the generic level, outreach ministry to addicted people is done like outreach ministry to any target population—from blind or deaf people, to the medical or arts community, to a subculture or an ethnic minority language population: (1) Gather data and "intelligence" about the population. (2) Learn what other churches, in similar communities, are doing to reach and serve this population. (3) Build alliances with others who work with them, have bridges to them, and are concerned for them. (4) Deploy Christians from the population to minister with them. (5) Determine objectives, develop plans, provide the funds and leadership, and implement the plans through the complete management process.[32]

The "Underground Awakening"

The Recovery movement is already the "Underground Awakening" of this generation; more people are discovering the grace of God for the first time in Twelve Step groups than in evangelism programs! Whether churches choose to run with this movement or not will determine whether some churches have a future worth having. Most communities need many more recovery groups than are now available; the church is the only organization or institution that is positioned in every community to support the needed range and number of groups. Today, more churches than ever before offer recovery ministries. Less than 10 percent of churches feature recovery ministries, but we now find some such churches in almost every city.

On a recent trip to South Florida, I visited the Friday evening recovery ministry of Christ United Methodist in Fort Lauderdale, which has pioneered in outreach ministries since senior pastor Dick Wills helped the church crystallize a simple vision for ministry in three priority areas: (1) Introduce people to Jesus in positive ways. (2) Disciple people through small groups. (3) Relieve suffering.[33] Sixty or more people (white, black, and Hispanic) gathered for Celebrate Recovery as a praise band led the people in celebrating the power of God. Pastor Debbie McLeod spoke from Genesis 2 and 3; she exposed the Enemy as a big fat liar and gave several prescriptions for what to do with the HALT (hungry, angry, lonely, tired) needs that make addicted people vulnerable to the Liar.

She affirmed the presence of Christ to protect us, and she encouraged people to take the Third Step. When the service closed with the Serenity Prayer, people scattered into one of six Twelve Step groups.

Christ Church's people do not rely entirely on "attraction" to reach people in addiction; they meet people on the streets and in the prisons. In addition to the Friday night Celebrate Recovery service and groups, Christ Church offers Tuesday night AA, Alanon, and AWOL (Alcoholic Way of Life)—an advanced high-commitment study, involving more than two hundred people in recovery, that began in prisons in Canada. Debbie McLeod reports, "Eight of our church's lay pastors are ex-convicts!"

I spent Sunday north of Miami, with the Fulford United Methodist Church, where I became a Christian as a teenager in 1955. For more than a decade now, I wanted to learn about Fulford Church's ministry to addicted gamblers. Gamblers Anonymous meets at Fulford Church on Wednesday nights. They limit the group to about twenty-five because they have discovered that it is important that everyone speak at every meeting; they report that it is even more important (than in AA) that every recovering gambler have a sponsor.

I interviewed Harold, about seventy years old, who is one of the ministry's leaders, who now represents Florida on the national Gamblers Anonymous board. Harold started gambling at sixteen; he gambled for more than thirty years. Eventually, it cost him everything except his family—who insisted he start attending Gamblers Anonymous meetings. He started attending to pacify his wife, still denying he needed to go; it took him six months to own his problem—that "I lived for the endorphin rush that I only got from gambling, win or lose." Harold reports that, though he has been "clean" for twenty-two years, "I can still feel very guilty. But I give hospitality to many people who need to talk."

Damon Doyle, in his midthirties, is a leader in Fulford Church's Narcotics Anonymous ministry; one group meets Monday nights, another Tuesday nights. Damon's parents divorced when he was a child; he found "family" with other kids who understood his pain and taught him how to numb the pain with drugs. He dropped out of school, a cocaine addict, in the eighth grade; he "got high on something" almost every day for twenty years. Somehow, through the whole experience, Damon "always believed in Christ." He entered a residential recovery facility, where he discovered that Christ was using the meetings, where he could identify with and trust the other addicts, to speak to him. He was placed in a "three-quarter house" not far from Fulford Church. "I visited one day, and immediately I felt I belonged to this church." He found reasons to trust and bond with Fulford's pastor, Steve Hoffman, who is also in recovery.

When I met Damon, he had been clean for sixteen months. He reports he is still vulnerable: "That same dark voice still talks to me, sometimes." Damon attends at least two NA meetings every week—a small meeting where everyone can talk, and a big meeting "where you can feel the power." Damon also does recovery devotionals every morning and evening, stays close to his sponsor and his pastor, and invites other addicts to NA and to church. Damon feels as though he is "just now learning to live." His spiritual recovery has awakened a gift for writing poetry; I have gerrymandered some of Damon's lines to characterize Damon's pilgrimage:

I thought I was damaged beyond repair,
When I tried to walk, I would step into snares.
When I looked into the mirror, I saw reflection of a sinner,
I knew that death was near, for my face was getting thinner.
[The Evil One] had made me a leper, so ugly and so sickly,
So twenty years had gone by, all too very quickly.

He had sent many snakes into the grass,
Hissing at me and trying to bite my ass.
He is a master of clever disguise,
He had me believing all his lies.

I was just a child and really lost,
But I never lost faith in my Lord on the cross.
He offered me His unconditional love,
And, at last, He got through to me from above.
Now I know that I am in God's plans,
And He has chosen me as one of His lambs.
He watches me grow just like a flower,
I am so glad I chose Him as my Higher Power.
My faith in Him I feel with conviction,
He helps me be free from all my addiction.

He taught me how to shine my shoes,
And to bring cheer to people when they have the blues.
He taught me not to dig up dirt,
And never to say things to people that hurt.
He taught me that the flesh is weak,
And to be very careful before I speak.
He taught me to speak clearly and never to mumble,
To hold my head high but always stay humble.
He taught me how to dance to the beat,
And when it is time to move my feet.

Whenever I listen, he does teach
There is no one alive that He can't reach.
I thought my days were done, and I would die a drunken
*   fool,*
So I am blessed and honored to be used as His tool.
If you see him before me, please tell Him "Thanks—
For making my life complete and for filling in the blanks."

Most of the churches that miss out on the recovery movement may never experience such "miracles" in their midst.

Early in the history of AA, Father Ed Dowling, a Jesuit priest, became a strong friend of the movement and attended many meetings. Someone asked him why he was so involved, since he was not an alcoholic. The AA movement has often published his answer: "I went through all of my [eighteen years of] studies and didn't believe a damned thing. I came to believe by watching what happens to you people, the miracles, in Alcoholics Anonymous."

Ed Dowling got in line early! In the last half century, a lengthy parade of "regular" people have experienced faith as they saw "impossible" people becoming "miracle" people.

CHAPTER SIX

First Baptist Church, Leesburg, As a Church for Everyone

One would not expect to find a pioneering apostolic congregation in Leesburg, Florida. Leesburg, a citrus town of 18,000 to 20,000 people, is as culturally conservative a town as one would ever find. Although most of Central Florida experiences rapid population growth, Leesburg's many traditional restraints have permitted only glacierlike growth, though the surrounding Lake County population grows more rapidly. The population triples each winter as "snow birds" occupy vast tracts of (what were once called) mobile homes. "Innovation" is almost unknown in Leesburg. The gap between Leesburg's "upstanding citizens" and the socially marginal and "out of control" people is even wider than in most places. So one would not predict to find, in Leesburg, one church baptizing 250 to 300 new Christians each year, averaging over 2,000 in attendance, and which has grown to over 7,200 members by reaching "all the people we can find that no other church seems to want."

To "All the People We Can Find That No Other Church Seems to Want"

Pastor Charles Roesel accepted a call from Leesburg's First Baptist Church in 1976. Within months, attendance doubled from three hundred to six hundred, and the church experienced a momentum that encouraged its leaders to imagine the future they believed God wanted and to get very serious about outreach. Roesel used his preaching to awaken the people's desire "to reach all sorts of people"; his approach was expository preaching from passages in the Bible, "so they would have to know they were arguing with God!" Roesel also wanted his people to rely more consciously on the Holy Spirit, so they would risk more; citing Andy Anderson, Roesel observes that "the average church could do almost all its doing if God did not even exist."

First Baptist Church's vision emerged gradually; but by the mid-1980s, they were serving and reaching sharecroppers, migrant workers, neglected people, homeless people, unwed mothers, addicted people, at-risk children and youth, and abused women, as well as artistically talented people and up-and-outer people with some wealth and political power.

The church's outreach to "all sorts of people" did not emerge static free. For instance, an attorney once protested the church's shifting agenda: "I resent my wife and children having to walk past people like that to get to church." The church lost that family, and others, but most of the people caught the vision, and many contributed to it. Today, the church involves over fourteen hundred laity in over seventy outreach ministries. Many of the outreach ministries take place in the church's 32,000 square-foot Ministry Village; many other outreach ministries are offered across the city. The church's ministries engage a wide range of people's physical, emotional, and spiritual needs. The church, in a brochure, interprets the dynamic relationship between service and witness by quoting Dietrich Bonhoeffer:

> To allow the hungry to remain hungry would be blasphemy against God and one's neighbors. It is for the love of Christ, which belongs as much to the hungry man as to myself, that I share my bread with the homeless. If the hungry man does not attain to faith, then the fault falls on those who refuse him bread. To provide the hungry man with bread is to prepare the way for the coming of grace.

First Baptist Church characterizes its approach as "ministry evangelism." Ron Johnson, professor of evangelism at Mercer University's McAfee School of Theology in Atlanta, first alerted me to Leesburg's experiment; he calls it "ministry-based evangelism."

The "Roesel Revolution"

This local revolution would not have occurred without the catalytic leadership of Charles Roesel; indeed, Roesel's life experiences and his distinctive views especially prepared him for leading and forming a missional church. Roesel experienced poverty and indebtedness for years; so, he reflects, he understands people struggling to make ends meet. "I identify with them. I can see and feel life through their eyes. I have no reason to feel superior." When Roesel sees people barely coping, he recalls, "There, but by the grace of God, go I." Roesel's "confessional preaching" seems to connect with "hard-living people." He shares, in his preaching, enough of his own problems, temptations, and (especially) anxieties for people to feel he understands them. "I'm a worrier, so I attract worriers."

Theologically, Charles Roesel believes that ministry to marginal and outcast people is central to following Jesus. He observes that first-century Jewish religion functioned to serve the good people and

> to keep out "undesirables." A Gentile could break into the system only with great effort. . . . Relatively few persons took the initiative to do this, and Jewish religious leaders certainly made no concerted effort to reach out to Gentiles with redemptive love. These leaders were far more inclined to put persons in derogatory categories than to tell them of God's love. They spoke of sinners, Samaritans, tax collectors, people of the land, and Gentile dogs. They erected tall barriers to keep out such persons. . . . Part of their hatred of Jesus grew from the fact that He was unaffected by the barriers they had erected. Gentiles, Samaritans, tax gatherers, prostitutes, lepers, women—all experienced Jesus' redemptive love. He obviously did not share the Jewish leaders' religious exclusivism. Nor was His ministry calculated to preserve the status quo.[1]

Charles Roesel is also driven by deep convictions about "the priesthood of all believers." He believes that the Holy Spirit "gifts" people for specific significant ministries and that the widely used "inventories" for helping people discover their gifts are useful. Ministry, however, requires both giftedness and consecration, so Roesel invites people, over time, to the "fivefold surrender" that empowers laity to be world changers:

- the mind surrendered to be an intelligent Christian
- the heart surrendered to be a loving Christian
- the body surrendered to be a useful Christian
- the spirit surrendered to be a dynamic Christian
- the will surrendered to be an obedient Christian.[2]

This perspective now backs more than fourteen hundred of First Baptist Church's people in specific, serious, significant, avocational ministries involving, typically, a time commitment of five to ten hours each week. First Baptist Church's lay ministries include such ministries as pastoral care, counseling, baptizing, serving communion, and funerals—ministries that laypeople never get to do in "normal" churches. The church's three-session new member orientation helps every new church member discover his or her spiritual gifts and get into some ministry.

The church even deploys people in some ministries *before* they belong or believe. Bill and Susan O'Brien accepted the ministry of tutoring people for their GED (the high school diploma equivalency exam) before either believed. Bill dropped out of school in the tenth grade. A woman later befriended him and coached him for his GED; this time he "took to learning" and eventually became a CPA. Initially, Bill accepted the challenge of tutoring GED aspirants out of gratitude for what the woman once did for him; but through involvement in the ministry, and the church's worship, study, and fellowship, one day he discovered he believed, and he accepted the invitation to commit. Susan was raised, with no church background, by an atheist stepfather. When she and Bill moved to Leesburg, their son began going to First Baptist Church. Someone told Susan that the church's Men's Residence could use her strength in tutoring math. Susan, too, discovered that the faith is even more caught than taught.

"Proactive Outreach" Begins, and Then Multiplies

First Baptist Church's proactive outreach began in 1979, when the church declared all of Leesburg's nursing homes and homebound senior adults within the First Baptist parish! Charles and Bonnie Keesling moved to Leesburg from Atlanta to head the ministry's expansion. They now deploy seventy-two volunteers to visit five hundred to seven hundred senior adults each week, and they now minister in eight nursing homes. Lay teams lead twenty- to thirty-minute worship services in each nursing home; and they visit, read the Scriptures, and pray with residents who cannot make the service. They often engage in ministry with family members of residents. In recent years, this ministry has extended to hospitals, including ministering to people in intensive care.

First Baptist's seniors' ministry has dispelled the myth that "older people are resistant; if they haven't become Christians by now, they never will." From this ministry, fifty to ninety older people accept Christ each year. Baptism (by immersion), however, is no longer part of the ministry to nursing home converts. Charles Keesling explains: "We baptized a 190-pound lady, and we almost drowned her; so we don't do that anymore!" (I resisted the temptation to offer a "Methodist" solution to this problem!) Older people who accept Christ but cannot attend church are not usually added to First Baptist's membership role, in part because the church believes it is important for the church to be in ministry with people who could never benefit the church, institutionally. The lay teams also lead twenty to thirty graveside services each year.

A team of laity joins with Ken Scrubbs, the church's African American Minister of Community Relations, in a "Saturday Sunday School" outreach to children in lower-income neighborhoods. Several hundred children travel on church buses for the Saturday morning experience. Children meet in one of three age groups: four year olds and kindergartners, first through fifth grades, and sixth grade and older. Since there are seldom enough workers for all the children to have a small group experience, the children meet only in one of the three large groups. Leaders learned quickly that the program needs to be entertaining and needs to involve the children to retain their interest. The program employs drama and puppet skits, slide and overhead projector presentations, and contemporary appealing music to introduce themes of the gospel and the Christian lifestyle. A child's bus driver serves as the child's pastor, the group on the bus as the child's support group— often a social alternative to gang membership. The bus driver, with a team of several other members who ride the bus and befriend the children, also befriends each family; entire families have been reached.

Several years ago, with the help of a grant, First Baptist Church started a 3,000-square-foot medical clinic for people who lack medical insurance, cannot pay for full medical services, and do not qualify for Medicare or Medicaid. About fifteen physicians and fifty other volunteers (nurses, paramedical, and clerical people) have served about 450 patients per month; a recent expansion of the facility permits the clinic to serve eight hundred to nine hundred people per month. Both patients and medical personnel have become Christians through this ministry.

The church finds ways to reach people who are "up and out." Since 1997, the Daystar Academy of Music and Performing Arts has targeted Leesburg's most "talented" children and youth. Under the direction of Ali Dickson, a vocalist and music educator, a part-time faculty of eighteen now mentors over 250 children and youth in voice, dance, theater, piano, trumpet, violin, guitar, saxophone, drums, and a range of other instruments, performing arts, and visual arts. Ali Dickson reports that Daystar Academy proposes "to build a fine arts program that will help students develop their skills to the glory of God. We strive to present positive Christian alternatives that convey the message of the gospel and enhance the climate for evangelism." With the Academy, First Baptist joins a promising evangelical movement to produce people who can communicate with pre-Christian people through the arts.

Dickson reports that 70 percent of the Academy's students are not from First Baptist families; about 50 percent report no active church affiliation. Not many children and their families have become people of faith through their involvement with the Academy, but Dickson reports, "We believe that many are now in process of becoming Christians."

First Baptist Church began a Christian school in the 1989–90 school year—beginning with kindergarten and first grade—that now serves children through the eighth grade. The school is an outreach ministry of the church; so, unlike most Christian schools, First Baptist does *not* require that children, or their parents, be Christians to enroll in the school. In a typical year, about 40 percent of the newly enrolled children do not come from an active Christian family; some children, with their families, become Christians every year.

"Ministry Village"

The church offers a range of ministries through a complex of buildings known as Ministry Village. The Village's staff executive is Dan McCormick—a member for twenty-one years—who, midcareer, sold the family business and moved "from success to significance." The Ministry Village has its own budget—separate from the church's regular budget. Several other churches (including a Presbyterian church and an Assembly of God church) and many people and organizations support the Ministry Village. Walt Disney World, Albertsons, and Publix donate much of the food for its programs. The Village's ministries serve more than four thousand people each year. The people who are resident in one of the ministries, however, are integrated into the life of the church—worship services, Sunday school classes, small groups, fellowship, and even ministries. Although staff people manage the residential units, lay people lead most of the specific ministries.

First Baptist Church began a Rescue Mission in 1982, providing food and shelter for transient men. The Rescue Mission has evolved into the Men's Residence, which now provides support, training, counseling, and the Twelve Step process for recovery from addiction. The staff leader of the Men's Residence is Jay Walsh who, earlier in his life, joined his Miami-area church in ministry with the Miami Rescue Mission. Later, living in Leesburg, Walsh reflects, "The ministries drew me to this church. It was almost like God called us here. They were doing what Jesus would have done." The residence houses thirty men, including six men who now have outside jobs but have stayed to help other men in recovery. The ministry aims to place men in jobs, apartments, and independent living. The ministry, Walsh reports, "takes broken empty men who have lost their sense of dignity, and we hope they find the dignity that God wants them to have through Christ." Men's length of time in residency varies—from a week or two to several months. The Men's Residence is able to serve about two hundred men each year.

Upon completing the program, about 30 percent of the men stay in the Leesburg area; 70 percent of those remain active in First Baptist Church, and, one lay volunteer told me, "They funnel a lot of energy into the church." "Bob" stands as one of the mission's inspiring cases. He came to the program estranged from his family, in trouble with the law, having lost everything. He completed the program ten years ago; he now owns a company and serves the church as a deacon. Some men do later relapse, particularly men who move away after completing the program. Twenty volunteers provide most of the specific ministries, from anger management and money management, to Twelve Step work, Bible study, and physical disciplines. The volunteers subscribe to certain "principles of ministry"—such as showing love and unconditional acceptance at all times and maintaining the client's responsibility for his recovery.

The Ministry Village features the Children's Shelter Home—for neglected and abused children. The Home provides a loving and supportive residence and meals, clothing, and medical attention for sixteen children in transition—until they can be placed back in their homes, or into foster homes or adoptive homes. In 2000, the church opened the Teen Shelter Home.

The Ministry Village's Benevolence Ministry serves the largest population—almost eight thousand people in a recent year. The program provides food, gasoline, rent assistance, electricity and prescription vouchers, clothing, and financial counseling as people need. With each person, the volunteers do an assessment, and they work to build friendships and to share some good news. Some recipients have responded and are now Christians; several now serve as volunteers in the Benevolence Ministry. Others do not respond beyond accepting the immediate help; some cannot even be found later.

The Pregnancy Care Center serves twelve hundred women and teens each year. The Ministry Village newsletter describes two typical cases:

- A fifteen-year-old comes in pregnant and confused. She has been molested by two consecutive stepfathers, her mother does not want her, she has no place to go, and the father of the unborn child is in jail. Just try to imagine how low she perceives her self-worth to be.
- Another fifteen-year-old comes into the PCC, having been raped by her stepfather at age twelve. She raises a child by that stepfather along with another child by a young fellow who does not respond to the plea to be responsible. Now, she is pregnant again. She does not know why she continues to live the lifestyle that causes so much confusion in her life and that does not allow lasting relationships, which she so desperately needs.

From its pro-life philosophy, the Center makes women and girls aware of the options before them, options besides abortion and including adoption counseling and referrals. (The Center has facilitated over one hundred adoptions in fourteen years.) The Center offers pregnancy tests; Lamaze, nutrition, parenting, and financial planning classes; diapers; baby clothes; baby beds; car seats; and counseling. When not terminating a pregnancy would cause problems in a girl's home situation, the church provides a nurturing "shepherding home" to live in.

The Pregnancy Care Center also offers a ministry of counseling to women who have had abortions, who now feel they did wrong. The church advertises this ministry in the city. The flyer reads (in part):

ARE YOU SUFFERING FROM
- RELATIONSHIP PROBLEMS
- EATING DISORDERS
- ABUSE OF ALCOHOL OR DRUGS
- LACK OF SELF-ESTEEM
- DEPRESSION
- SLEEPING DISORDERS

If the answer is yes and you have had an abortion, You may be suffering from **POST-ABORTION SYNDROME**

CARE (Counseling for Abortion and Related Experiences) is offering a recovery class for Post-abortal women that is confidential. There is no charge. Be free of the guilt, shame, sorrow, loneliness, and regret which often appear **years** after the abortion.

The flyer includes the Monday evening, ten-week schedule for the sessions. With this information, women come for help at their own initiative.

Wanda Kohn, a devoted volunteer, leads this ten-week, eleven-session recovery process. She observes that many women "ask forgiveness from God, but they still won't forgive themselves and beat themselves up. If a woman still harbors anger, hurt, bitterness, shame, despair, and guilt, then she needs to confront these issues in her life, so she can experience the freedom and truth of God's forgiveness and come to a place where she can forgive herself."

The process begins by stating three conditions for recovery through the course: A woman must (1) genuinely desire to be restored, (2) be willing to trust the Scriptures, and (3) commit to completing the course. Early sessions help each woman clarify and tell her story, and the story of her abortion within her larger story, and hear one another's stories. The women discover how the experience has impacted them physically, emotionally, behaviorally, and spiritually. Later sessions help each woman identify and work through the feelings of grief, anger, denial, depression, and guilt that sabotage their spirits. Each session features promises from the Scriptures, such as "I know the plans I have for you, says the Lord, plans for your welfare and not for harm, to give you a future with hope" (Jer. 29:11). Near the end, the women are encouraged to pray that God would reveal the gender and name of the baby. A pastor joins Wanda Kohn in leading a memorial service; each woman is given a red rose wrapped in Baby's Breath fern. Kohn reports that the experiences of praying for the baby's name and gender and the memorial service are often the most healing part of the process.

Wanda Kohn started offering classes for women in jail who had their children taken away. She has led over two hundred women through that experience; a dozen have become Christians. Wanda Kohn and several other members at First Baptist have discovered "a wide open field— offering classes in jails!"

Insights from the Women's Care Center

The ministry of the Village's Women's Care Center serves as a window for understanding many similar ministries.

Since 1989, the Center has served as a response to the fastest growing segment of the nation's homeless population—single women with children, often abused, abandoned, or addicted, with nowhere else to go. The facility provides residence for up to twelve weeks, and a range of ministries, for seventeen women and their small children. In addition to room and board, the Center provides child care, financial assistance, medical care, vocational training, help in finding employment and permanent housing, and the power of a supportive community. A brochure tells us, "The Women's Care Center exists to meet the needs of homeless women and children—physical, emotional, and spiritual."

The Women's Care Center's director is Carol Barber, who grew up in a dysfunctional alcoholic family and became like her parents. A flower child of the 1960s, she spent years in the countercultural hippie movement. She'd been a Christian for three years when she and her husband moved to Leesburg and joined First Baptist Church. Her back ground gives her an understanding of, and credibility with, the people she now serves. Most of the Center's women, Barber reflects, "come from an exploitative world and a self-destructive lifestyle that has taken away any dignity and self-respect. They are pretty beaten down when they come here, but they clean up pretty well, and their self-worth comes, and their countenance changes—gradually!"

Almost every woman comes to the Center with multiple issues and with some resistance to being helped. The Center, necessarily, interviews prospective residents and has to be somewhat selective; they select women who appear ready for change, and they are not staffed to help women with extreme mental illness. They develop a case plan for each woman; then a woman has to be working her plan to stay. Carol Barber noticed that the women are aware that a church supports the Center, "so we represent God to them. How they perceive me influences how they see God." Fortunately, Barber says, "if they experience unconditional love from us, it is much more than they are used to." The love they experience has to be "tough love, with consequences. We allow them to fail, in a safe environment. We pick them up, forgive them, and support them, and they learn to move on." Barber has found two themes repetitively useful: (1) Agree with them, "Life is *not* always fair." (2) Inform and remind them, "God has a plan."

The church's body of insights gained from this ministry would be useful to many churches and many ministries. The Center teaches all volunteers five guidelines for engaging in useful ministry with this population: (1) Help a woman identify her options; do not decide for her what she should do. (2) Help a woman determine the steps she should take; do not take the steps for her. (3) Help a woman discover her own strength; do not rescue her and leave her still vulnerable. (4) Help a woman take responsibility for her life; do not take responsibility for her. (5) Help a woman find a new life in Christ; do not try to reform the old life. Volunteers and staff have to reinforce persistently "the principle of the client's personal responsibility. While we . . . provide temporary relief to women in crisis, we must not make relief the permanent response. The primary goal is to share our lives, our time, our skills, our energy and the gospel in ways that empower clients to break out of the cycle of sin and destitution, and to be free to assume responsibility for their own needs."

The Center has developed useful guidelines for the ministry of evangelism with this population: (1) Don't assume a woman's lifestyle, behavior, or speech signals unresponsiveness to the gospel. Conduct or appearance may be calculated to intimidate or give an air of self-sufficiency when, in fact, the individual feels insecure or frightened. Volunteers are encouraged (2) prayerfully to discern when a "teachable moment is present" and (3) to modify one's presentation of the gospel "for each individual's needs."

(4) Be willing to sow in the client's life, even if you don't see the person come to faith in Jesus. You may be one in a chain of people whom God will use to draw her to Godself. (5) Trust God to convict people and to give them faith and life.

The Center has identified several relational qualities that contribute to a volunteer's effectiveness in this ministry: (1) *Empathy* involves the sensitivity and skill to "think with" *and* "feel with" the other person, to communicate back to the woman what she is thinking and feeling, and thereby to experience *identification* with her. (2) *Genuineness*, involving appropriate honesty, transparency, openness, and vulnerability, helps create the *friendship* that is more transformative than a mere professional/client relationship. (3) *Unconditional acceptance* "means to affirm and care for the person, apart from her lifestyle—not condoning the woman's sinful behavior, but accepting her in spite of it." (4) *Humility* "is the ability to recognize your own limits as well as strengths." The need for humility applies not only to staff and volunteers, but also to the whole ministry. Humility involves *not* presuming to offer services for which God has not provided the human and financial resources, and not feeling guilty for the services you cannot provide. The Women's Care Center, for instance, would like to offer psychiatric therapy within its ministries, but cannot.

Carol Barber has learned that flexibility is required in this ministry, for the simple reason that "nothing goes exactly like you planned." This reality is reflected on the "Office Hours" sign posted on Barber's office door:

Carol's Office Hours:
Open most days about 8:00 or 9:00
Occasionally as early as 7:00
But some days as late as 12:00 or 1:00.
I leave about 5:30 or 6:00

Occasionally about 4:00 or 5:00
But sometimes as late as 9:00 or 10:00.
Some days I am not here at all
But lately I've been here just about all the time.
Except when I'm somewhere else. But I should be here
    then, too!

Director

The Women's Care Center receives most of the women by referral—from social service and law enforcement agencies, jails, mental health centers, drug treatment programs, other churches, family, and friends. While the women are in the program, most of them (1) commit, or recommit, their lives to Christ and (2) become involved in First Baptist Church (in either order). Upon completion, they are such a mobile population that the Center lacks the data to know the rate of long-term successes and relapses. Some women, having failed or relapsed, return to the Center for another period. Many women stay, and thrive, in the Leesburg area and First Baptist Church. About half of the voices in the 8:00 A.M. service's sixty-voice choir are visible "trophies" of the Women's Care Center and the Men's Residence. The Center has a Sunday school class for its women; each week, two or three "alumnae" return to the class to encourage the women now in the program.

Although every case, and every story, is unique, "Kelly's" case represents many. Kelly, at thirty, was a single mother with two small children, surviving on welfare. Following an arrest, she was admitted to the Women's Care Center. She recovered her self-esteem and sense of purpose. She started working as a waitress while still at the Center; soon her children were no longer supported by Aid to Families with Dependent Children. Today, she says, "I work like a dog." She and her two children now live in a small rental house. Though she still receives food stamps, she rejected federally subsidized housing because, "I don't need it as badly as some other people." She recently discovered, to her delight, that she owed the IRS $400 in income tax!

First Baptist Church's Emerging Future

Space does not permit a full report of most of First Baptist Church's many lay ministries. The people lead at least a dozen other notable outreach ministries, including bereavement and grief ministries, hospital ministries, and a range of prison ministries, ministries with single adults and senior adults, ministries with deaf people and preliterate people, groups for cancer support and divorce recovery, ministries in mobile home parks, and classes on needs from nutrition, to infant care, to financial planning.

The church continues to plan and launch new outreach ministries. For instance, First Baptist recently employed Pastor George Gonzales, from Puerto Rico, to plant a Spanish-speaking congregation and lead other ministries to and with Hispanic peoples. Gonzales's wife, Ruth, a nurse, is beginning ministries for people with AIDS. The church now plans to build, or acquire, a retirement home for senior adults who cannot afford the other retirement homes in the Leesburg area. The church is exploring ways to get in intentional ministry with people who have mental illnesses.

The church recently launched what is, arguably, the church's single most audacious experiment in outreach. It began when Charles Roesel was visiting with a woman who was once a community pillar, who then engaged in some tragic choices that made her a public scandal; now, years later, she was wishing for a church that offers hope and love to people like her. Roesel, with several lay Christians, recalled the names of a number of people in Leesburg "with scars in their background, who once did something horrible, who are widely shunned. Many upstanding citizens won't even speak to them; they don't fit, anywhere, in polite Leesburg society." Four laypeople volunteered to sponsor a new Sunday school class to reach and involve Leesburg's best-known "misfits." The church's deacons gave them fervent prayer support. Two months ago (from this writiing), the class began with four new people; last Sunday, the class welcomed sixteen. Several have never before been involved in a church. Several are already inviting others. The new people are bonding with one another, and with the church, even more than the leaders had expected; a second class for "publicly scandalized misfits" is projected.

"Positioning" First Baptist Church, Leesburg, Within an Apostolic Perspective

We can "position" Leesburg's First Baptist Church within the multiple apostolic perspectives.

The leaders and people of First Baptist Church are remarkably clear about the priority of evangelism. Although they are most noted for their outreach ministries, they know that they leave people ultimately impoverished if they do not experience the forgiveness of sins, reconciliation with God, and second birth, and become followers of Jesus Christ, seeking his will for their lives and the world. Charles Roesel reminds the people that Jesus invites his disciples to "follow me, and I will make you fishers of men." So, Roesel reasons, "If we are not fishers of men, we are not following Jesus."

Roesel and his people acknowledge that "the methodology for accomplishing this continues to be debated," but the church has discovered that, with increasing numbers of people, witness alone does not reach them and may even be counterproductive. With more and more people, you get into ministry with them first, and into friendship and conversation. Then, when they are far enough along in the chain of experiences toward faith, a time of loving "confrontation," in which the gospel is explained (again) and a response is invited, is often appropriate, and necessary. Roesel defines the church's main business as "a mission of evangelism that involves ministry to the total person."

The church is clear that fidelity to the Great Commission involves mission locally, regionally, and globally. So First Baptist has planted several new churches and has sent hundreds of its members to support these new churches. In foreign missions, First Baptist tithes its gross income to the Southern Baptist Foreign Mission Board and also supports seven missionaries in the service of the para-church mission agency, New Tribes Mission. The church knows the reproductive value of having members with short-term mission experience, so the church deploys several teams of laity each year, for several weeks, where they contribute to projects, support the national church, relate to indigenous people, and speak for the Christian gospel. Roesel recalls that "in the last ten years, or so, our people have helped build over sixty schools, hospitals, chapels, and other structures in Africa, Romania, Brazil, or elsewhere." During the week I visited First Baptist Church, most of the men experiencing recovery in the Men's Residence were unavailable for interviews; they were in South Florida, building a school for Seminole Indian children.

The church is clear that effective grassroots Christianity is a lay movement, that all twice-born Christians are "gifted" for ministry, that most churches need to "loose the laity" for their ministries and mission. I have never observed a church in which more ministries that matter— including difficult and complex ministries requiring sophisticated understanding—were entrusted to laypeople. Moreover, I never detected the assumption that the choice of a layperson for a ministry represents Plan B. The church believes that the gift-based deployment of laity is usually Plan A, that most ministries would *not* be done better if done by someone who is ordained. Indeed, the church's leaders are not satisfied that only 1,400 out of 7,200 members are involved in serious ministries.

Critique for an Even Greater Mission

Although Leesburg's First Baptist Church already "practices what I preach" as much as any church I know, some critique is appropriate, at four points:

Recovery Ministries

Most churches are like the lifeguard who is only interested in rescuing people floundering in shallow water near the beach. I experienced First Baptist Church like a lifeguard who is pumped to rescue drowning people from the deepest far-out waters, but may ignore people struggling to cope in shallower waters. That is, on a "seriousness scale" of 1 to 10, the church's men's and women's residences serve people whose addiction problem is a "10," and they serve the local alumni of the two residences. However, the church comparatively ignores the addicted people whose (current) level of seriousness is less than 10. Many people, of course, are in the grips of alcohol, drug, sexual, or gambling addiction, but they are still "making it," while leading dysfunctional lives of quiet desperation. With the church's reputation, I expected (say) a range of twenty to thirty recovery groups meeting each week, and I expected many stories of victory from addiction, apart from the intensive ministries of the Men's Residence and the Women's Care Center.

Although no church is obligated to live up to a seminary professor's expectations, Leesburg's hard-living people—often the same people whose children attend the Saturday Sunday school, who come themselves to the church's medical clinic, clothes closet, or food pantry—need support for recovering sobriety and sanity. Addiction is the greatest under-acknowledged epidemic in North America; there are never enough *good* Twelve Step meetings in cities like Leesburg, and serving that population is fully congruent with First Baptist's local mission. To the church's credit, it has positive regard for AA's "big book," and the Men's Residence, at least, helps its men through the Twelve Step recovery process. But churches like First Baptist need strong intentional alliances with the wider recovery movement, and the occasional "drifting" of the recovery movement reveals its need for involvement with churches.

Indeed, First Baptist Church owes it to the residents and alumni of their men's and women's residential missions to ground them in the Twelve Steps and recovery literature, to introduce their men and women to the wider recovery movement, and to help them begin networking with other people in recovery. Why? The men's and women's facilities' leaders report that, although the relapse rate of their people who stay in Leesburg is low, the relapse rate of people who scatter to other communities is much higher. If their dispersed alumni were prepared to find the local recovery community and get a sponsor and continue working their program, fewer would relapse. In most communities, after all, there are more likely to be AA meetings than churches like Leesburg's First Baptist Church.

Small Groups

First Baptist Church does not involve as many people in small group life as I expected. The one published book featuring the church, *Meeting Needs, Sharing Christ*,[3] devotes a chapter to the power of community and fellowship in shaping people for abundant life, ministry, and witness. All disciples need *koinonia* in the "deep sense of belonging to one another." Roesel and Atkinson observe, "If God's people are to witness and minister to a lost and hurting world, koinonia must be the sustaining context in which they find their strength and will to do so."[4] The authors are clear that the experience of Christian fellowship is necessary for assimilating new people, nurturing people, and even healing people's spirits. Furthermore, they are clear that all this takes place in small groups, or, for most people, it doesn't take place at all. So, they say, a church needs to involve its people in discovery groups, support groups, Sunday school classes, and service groups ("composed of those who work in a particular area of ministry"), in which they minister to one another.

I discovered some deterioration in the church's small group life since the mid-1990s, when the book was written. The Sunday school is still strong, and many of the classes are small enough for the small group mutual ministry experience. The service groups are still operative and are meaningful and powerful for the people involved. But the number of discovery groups and support groups, and the number of people involved in them, is only a fraction of the number of groups and involved people in the early and mid-1990s. I searched for an explanation for this decline and found an astonishingly simple one: The Director of Christian Education, who administered the small groups program, left the staff in 1994 and has not been replaced. Without that leadership, the network of discovery groups and support groups gradually declined.

I concluded that this decline in two of the four expressions of small group life stands as a significant, if subterranean, reason for the fact that the church has grown less in recent years, has baptized somewhat fewer people, and has the same number of people involved in ministries today (about 1,400) as when the book was written. I submit that the church cannot afford to wait for the right Director of Christian Education to become available. Small group life is important enough to hire a part-time director for that, or to place it in another staff member's leadership; the Bible does not specify that only a "director of Christian education" can lead a small group movement! Indeed, First Baptist Church's small group life is even more important to the church's mission and future than it once perceived. Like many churches that are serious about mission, one day it will move from being "a church with small groups" to "a church *of* small groups," and it will become even more explosive in its outreach.

Cultural Relevance

First Baptist Church, probably reflecting the small city's conservative culture, has not sufficiently discovered the revelatory power of "cultural relevance," or "Indigenous Christianity," in their mission field. For years, the church offered three worship services—a "traditional" service at 9:45, a (not very) "blended" service at 11:00, and a traditional gospel Sunday evening service at 6:00. After years of (minority) advocacy for a "contemporary" service, the leadership reluctantly agreed to a "nontraditional" service offered at 8:00 A.M.—a time slot that, some leaders assumed, would kill the experiment because unchurched people are not noted for getting up early for church! To almost everyone's surprise, the 8:00 nontraditional service quickly became the service with the largest attendance! (This 8:00 A.M. alternative service features the music of the Brooklyn Tabernacle Choir. One day, thousands of churches will offer an alternative service, featuring Brooklyn Tabernacle choir music.)

The leaders still have not quite caught on and are still discussing the *possibility* of one or more contemporary services. *When* (not *if*) the leaders discover that each people's culture is the medium of God's revelation to them, and start taking indigenous Christianity seriously, they will add a couple of contemporary services and a recovery service and, in time, ministries in other ethnic-minority languages bedsides Spanish. When, during the weekend will they schedule more services? They will learn from the schedule pioneering of some other churches that Friday and Saturday evenings are often available, that Sunday noon or early afternoon is a good time, and that a second service could be held concurrently in another part of their facility. Furthermore, they may start "counting" the services their people already lead in nursing homes, trailer parks, and other venues.

Church Structure

An examination of First Baptist Church reveals that it has two structures—the church itself and the Ministry Village—each with its own organization, budget, and so forth. The first unit sponsors the second and is good about welcoming its people. However, the Ministry Village is the unit that is organized for outreach. Essentially, as the church staff commented during my visit, the church itself is a traditional program-based design church that is primarily organized to serve members. To its credit, the church is more committed to outreach than most traditional churches, and its passion for lay ministry is a wonderful "deviation" from the traditional local church paradigm. Essentially, however, it functions more like a traditional congregation ("attend church, attend Sunday school, attend programs") than an apostolic congregation. *That* is why it observed the attrition of its discovery groups and support groups and did not perceive this loss more seriously than it did.

So some critique of this church is possible, and even desirable, for its greater faithfulness and effectiveness. I feel free to publish this critique of the church, however, because I have enormous confidence in the church. When they see what will lead to greater mission, they will do it! Indeed, the church's leaders have already responded to each point in this critique since I sent them an early draft of this chapter. Furthermore, such observations should *not* detract from what the church is already achieving in its mission to "unlikely" people, or from the most important single lesson that any church can learn from First Baptist Church. As Charles Roesel reflects, "If it can happen in Leesburg, it can happen anywhere!"

CHAPTER SEVEN

Witness Through Ministry, Hospitality, and Conversation

Jesus' question in Luke 18:8 implied the Great Commission that he later made explicit; his question revealed how the faithfulness and effectiveness of his movement would be appraised: "When the Son of Man comes, will he find faith on earth?"

Jesus expressed this mandate in many ways. He invited his first disciples to follow him and become "fishers" of men and women (Mark 1:17). He commissioned us to "proclaim the good news to the whole creation" (Mark 16:15), to be his "witnesses in Jerusalem, Judea, Samaria, and to the ends of the earth" (Acts 1:8), to "make disciples of all nations" (Matt. 28:19). He identified us as his "ambassadors" (2 Cor. 5:20), through whom a reconciling God will appeal to people. Jesus lived, taught, died, arose, sent, and ascended, that people might know the reconciliation with God and the life for God and others that are experienced by grace through faith. As Leander Keck has often reminded church leaders, "The gospel is the only thing we have to offer to the world that it doesn't already have."

The answer to Jesus' question substantially depends upon his people. His church has ignored the mandate in more generations than has obeyed it. In this generation, many churches have rediscovered their main business, but, for either of two reasons, they do not know how to go about fulfilling their apostolic mission. First, in some denominations and traditions, many of today's church leaders were not mentored in outreach by the predecessor generation. Once upon a time, their tradition sent out many missionaries, and planted many churches and local churches lived to find lost people; but this has not been the driving agenda within living memory.

The second reason stems from a greatly changed, and changing, world: Other denominations and traditions have done mission, church planting, and evangelism within living memory, but the world has changed so much that, often, we cannot do it the ways our predecessors did. For instance, the old colonial approach to exporting culturally Western Christianity everywhere is now resisted almost everywhere; but much of the world is very receptive to a postcolonial, collaborative, indigenous approach to mission. Again, the inherited church planting approach that had judicatories planting churches—"new" churches that were mere clones of the older traditional churches—is a spent force; but the emergent patterns of churches planting alternative churches for people the established churches cannot reach—including many alternative congregations in established churches—are enormously promising. Furthermore, the inherited approaches to doing evangelism—from one-way gospel presentations, impersonal confrontation, and tract distribution, to revivals, camp meetings, and crusades—now gather negligible harvests compared to their heyday and, with many peoples in many places, are counterproductive.

The purpose of this chapter is to delineate the kind of apostolic evangelism that seems destined to take the place of the decreasingly effective approaches inherited from the nineteenth century. The first chapter drew from Paul's Corinthian letters to show some similarities between his context and ours, and to show some ways forward from these letters. This chapter draws from two passages in John's Gospel that reflect the ways the apostolic movement often did outreach, ways that informed the recovery of apostolic outreach in the later Celtic Christian movement, and ways that appear to be reemerging today.[1]

The First Disciples of Jesus (John 1:35-42)

The story of how three people—Andrew, Simon Peter, and an unnamed person (possibly John)—became Jesus' first disciples mirrors how many people become disciples today. We feature five such insights:

1. The Faith begins to spread when the faith's ambassadors penetrate the people's community and common life.

The story is clear that Jesus was not waiting in the synagogue for people to take the initiative to come to him; he was not the first-century equivalent of the counselor who hangs out a shingle and lets people schedule appointments. Rather, he was present, available, and making contacts in the city marketplace, where the people engaged in conversation and looked for Life. Three of Jesus' metaphors for his people—salt of the earth, light of the world, and leaven in the loaf—are all images of penetration. The parable of the soils (Mark 4 and its parallels) makes clear that the farmer "goes forth" to sow the seed. Every version of his Great Commission tells us to "go."

So the early apostolic bands took the gospel to the cities of the Mediterranean world. The later Celtic Christian movement took the initiative to every "barbarian" settlement it could find. Still later, John Wesley explained to his leaders that, to reach lost people, "we cannot expect them to seek *us*. Therefore we should go and seek *them*."[2] The apostolic congregation, by definition, is "sent"; so it does not wait for the people to come to the church.

That, however, is not what most churches do today. In North American cities, most of the *growing* churches are responding only to people who take the initiative to visit the church. The problem is that many people, even many seekers, will not initiate contact with a church; so we must take the initiative to contact them, on their turf. In many cities, however, it is hard to find churches that engage in proactive outreach, and even harder to find churches that care enough, and dare enough, to invade enemy territory.

2. The faith spreads person to person, along the lines of social networks.

The Christian faith does not usually spread between strangers, much less from mass crusades or televangelism; it spreads relationally, between people who know and trust one another and across kinship and friendship networks. John 1 models the faith spreading between friends, as John the Baptizer reports to Andrew and his other friend that Jesus is the promised "Lamb of God." John 1 also models the faith spreading between relatives, as Andrew finds his brother Simon and reports, "We have found the Messiah."

Donald McGavran observed that these two types of networks vary in their contagion from culture. In rural or traditional close-knit societies, kinship networks are more prolific; in more urban, cosmopolitan, individualistic societies, friendship networks are more prolific. Furthermore, McGavran observed that the kinship and friendship networks of *new* Christians are often the most prolific. Why? New Christians have more contacts with pre-Christian people than long-term members do. They still remember what life was like B.C.; many long-term members have forgotten. Their changed lives make the gospel very plausible to their peers. They still understand and speak the language of the people.

3. The "Ministry of Hospitality" fosters the people's discovery of faith.

The text features Andrew and his friend spending the afternoon with Jesus, where Jesus was staying, as his guests. The story thus models a twofold rhythm we often observe in effective evangelism today: The possibility begins when Christians take the initiative, penetrate the people's world, and engage them on their turf, in their comfort zone; the possibility continues as we invite, welcome, and include them in the life of the community of faith.

The Celtic Christian movement recovered the ancient ministry of hospitality; the monastic community's highest priority was welcoming and including seekers within its life. The Wesleyan movement reached people by welcoming them, before they had believed or experienced anything, into the life and worship of the Methodist classes and societies. John Finney observes that, to reach postmodern people today, "evangelism is about helping people belong so they can believe." Periodically, the church rediscovers that, for most people, the Christian faith is "more caught than taught."

4. The faith spreads, person to person, through the "Ministry of Conversation."

When John the Baptizer identified Jesus as the promised

Messiah, his two friends trailed Jesus to check it out. Jesus noticed them, and he asked, "What do you seek?" They asked, "Rabbi, where are you staying?" Jesus interpreted the question as a request for conversation, so he invited them to his place, where they spent the afternoon in conversation. Undoubtedly, the two men brought questions to the conversation. What they experienced with Jesus was *not* the brief one-way presentation that so many models of evangelism presuppose, but an honest, open-ended, two-way conversation ranging over several hours.[3]

From many vantage points, scholars keep rediscovering the power of conversation. The Sociology of Knowledge scholars, for instance, tell us that all people are "socialized" into a worldview, that is, a culturally scripted way of seeing life and the world. They tell us that, in a pluralistic society in which there are multiple worldviews, the mechanism that opens people of one worldview toward the possibility of adopting another worldview is conversation. Conversation is the major operating power in worldview conversion—not usually one conversation, but multiple conversations over time. The conversion process is complete when the convert has been socialized into the community that shares the new worldview.[4]

5. **People respond more to invitations than to ultimatums, often to multiple invitations, because becoming a Christian is a process that takes time.**

When Andrew asked, "Rabbi, where are you staying?" Jesus responded with more of an invitation than an answer: "Come and see." Notice, Jesus did not tell him to "turn or burn," or issue any kind of ultimatum. This exchange suggests, at least, what many churches have discovered: It takes time, typically months, for people to work through the possibility. Most people are no more prepared to become "instant Christians" than most young women are prepared to accept a marriage proposal on the first date.

This insight is best understood specifically. For instance, virtually no one "gets" the good news that we are justified by God's grace the first time one considers it. We are so culturally programmed to assume that top grades, job promotions, athletic championships, and salvation come by effort, merit, and worth, that something deep within us suggests that grace cannot possibly be true, or is too good to be true. We come to terms with it over time. Consider the gospel's other themes, such as the love, righteousness, and kingdom of God; a gospel of justification, second birth, and sanctification; and the invitation to live a new life of faith, hope, and love, a life in the community of Christ and by the will of God, and you can sense why it takes time to process enough of that for long enough to cross over the line and why we experience a lifetime of more processing, and deeper learning, after becoming a disciple. The first disciples were considering all of this for three years before they were clear that Jesus was "the Christ, the Son of the Living God." So churches rightly invite early seekers to "come and see," "check it out," "kick the tires and take it for a test drive," or "try it on for size to see if it fits." We invite people to begin, and continue, the process that leads to discovery and the gift of faith in God's good time.

Once again, a behavioral science perspective helps us see this reality from another vantage point. The Diffusion of Innovations tradition studies how new ideas, products, technologies, practices, causes, and movements "diffuse," or spread, within societies and from one society to another. This tradition, drawing from research in ten or more fields such as psychology, sociology, cultural anthropology, and communication theory, is especially interested in "the adoption process." What happens in a person's mind, scholars have asked, between the person's initial exposure to an idea and the person's "adoption" of the idea? They have identified a process that occurs in six approximate "stages":[5]

1. Awareness
2. Relevance
3. Interest
4. Trial
5. Adoption
6. Reinforcement

Diffusion theorists tell us that the adoption process takes time, typically months. Their point that, when a person adopts, the person needs postadoption reinforcing experiences for the adoption to "stick," has serious implications for radical outreach. Evangelism does not end with conversion. People need to be rooted in the faith and the community, socialized into a Christian worldview, and have validating experiences, for conversion to stick; without reinforcement, the person usually becomes a nominal Christian or reverts to the world.

The "Chain" of Experiences, and the Sources of the "Links"

Leaders of the Willow Creek Community Church talk about people becoming Christians as a result of a "chain of experiences" over time. The chain metaphor helps us see that every link in the chain is important and that the widespread evangelical assumption that only the last link really matters is dangerous and counterproductive. The metaphor helps us visualize that God is orchestrating a chain of experiences in the person's life to make faith possible and that our purpose, in any given moment, is to be used by God to provide one link in the chain.

The reality behind the chain metaphor is suggested in Paul's famous farming metaphor: "I planted, Apollos watered, and God gave the growth" (1 Cor. 3:6). My interviews with converts, and my studies of apostolic congregations, suggest that, today at least, the process is usually more protracted and complicated than that. We often have to clear away rocks and pull weeds and plow the field before we can plant; irrigation may be necessary. After planting, we often have to water, fertilize, and pull more weeds before we see signs of a crop, which we harvest still later. Fairly often, we get no crop the first time, and the gospel seed needs to be planted again, and perhaps again.

The nineteenth-century wisdom of Charles G. Finney, leader of the Second Great Awakening, reminds us that the experiences in the chain come from four sources.[6]

In Finney's model, one source of the experiences that move people along the chain is God. Converts often report experiences of the presence of God, the protection of God, or experiences of answered prayer, as moving them on in the process. Sometimes they perceived God's presence or answer at the time; more often through a rearview mirror. Finney is clear that although God is directly providing some of the experiences, God is also indirectly orchestrating a chain of experiences in the person's life to make the gift of faith possible in God's good time. Finney is also clear, however, that we cannot passively leave it up to God to reach people unilaterally; it is God's policy, Finney observed, to work through the three other sources.

Finney's second source of such experiences is Christians.[7] As Christians love people and believe in them and share good news and invite people, some of those efforts become links in the chain that leads to faith. A Christian might even provide a link unconsciously, as when a seeker observes a credible Christian serving, praying, or risking for someone else.

Finney's third source is Christian truth, which has its own kind of power. New converts typically report that one to several ideas, truths, or texts spoke to them deeply and would not leave their consciousness.

Finney's fourth source is the convert herself or himself.

Finney perceived seekers and converts as much more active agents in their own conversion than many theologians had allowed. So a convert-in-process may attend a small group, attend a worship service, read several books, pose questions to a Christian friend, study the Gospel of Luke, pray daily (even if they aren't sure there is a God who answers prayer), or (consistent with the trial stage in the adoption process, above) in specific situations or periods of time, act like they think a Christian would—to see if the clothes fit. And, throughout the process, the convert-in-process talks to himself—a thousand times. Often, the Holy Spirit reaches us through our "self-talk" most of all.

Some churches, today, have rediscovered the importance of the seeker's proactive involvement. For instance, Willow Creek Community Church grounds its people in the ministry of witness through conversation, a ministry typically involving many conversations with "Unchurched Harry" over time. Willow Creek believes that it is important to end each conversation by "leaving the ball in the seeker's court"; Harry needs to reflect between conversations. When Harry joins a Willow Creek seeker group, he notices that the leader usually declines to answer Harry's questions; the leader helps Harry access several sources to find Christian answers to his questions, and, at a later meeting, Harry presents to the group the insights he has discovered. Willow Creek schedules periodic forums, at which people can ask questions and church leaders will respond; but, in the seeker groups, the emphasis is on helping seekers discover and express the answers and insights from Christianity that are relevant to their questions and concerns.

Jesus and the Woman of Samaria (John 4)

John tells us, through certain cultural cues, that something very important is involved in Jesus' conversation

183

with the Samaritan woman he met at Jacob's well in Sychar, Samaria. A Jew engaged in a social conversation with a Samaritan was discouraged in Jewish customs. A man and a woman who did not already know each other engaging in social conversation was discouraged in both Jewish and Samaritan customs. Like a number of biblical characters, such as the rich young ruler, we do not know her name; but we do know much about her in this important account.

Notice four things about her, especially. First, she had ancestors who had known the God of Abraham; certain ancestors, such as Jacob, had been people of great faith. However, second, she was not substantially influenced by the Abrahamic faith. She had acquired some of the faith's language, such as the words "prophet" and "messiah"; but its deeper meaning had escaped her. Third, she was struggling in her personal life. Her life was not turning out according to any plan. We can infer that she came from a dysfunctional family, that she had a history of abuse, that she was possibly addicted or otherwise "out of control" at times. Since, in ancient Samaritan culture, a woman whose man would not marry her had no social standing, we know that she was marginalized and branded a "loser"; undoubtedly, she had a low sense of self-worth. However, fourth, she was a seeker, asking religious questions, though not always in the language of the Jewish religious tradition.

The woman at the well is an important biblical personality for the Western church today because, more and more, the Western world's cities are filled with people more or less like her. She stands as a biblical "prequel" of the "secular" people who, due to several centuries of secularization, now populate all of our communities in increasing numbers.[8]

Readers of my *How to Reach Secular People* may recall that, while I was a divinity school student, I spent the summer of 1962 at Muscle Beach, in Southern California. I engaged in ministry with a remarkable range of people—

such as bodybuilders and beatniks, surfers and sunbathers, prostitutes and homosexuals, drug addicts and drug pushers, and others. A dozen subcultures coexisted on the same turf, with little interchange between them; I seldom observed conversation between bodybuilders and beatniks, for instance. Each group thought of itself as very different from the others, and they were; but as far as I was concerned, almost all of them had one thing in common: They did not know what in the world I was talking about! They had no Christian memory, background, or vocabulary.

Gradually, I discovered four important insights about them that paralleled the Samaritan woman's profile. First, most of them had ancestors who were deeply involved in the Christian faith. They would report, say, a grandmother who'd been a pillar of a church back East or a great uncle who'd been a priest. Second, they themselves had never been substantially influenced by the Christian faith, though they knew a little jargon and a few Bible verses, such as "The Lord helps those who help themselves!" Third, they were often products of abuse and dysfunctional families; many were struggling in their personal lives or were vulnerable to addiction or experienced their life as sometimes out of control; many were marginalized and had a low sense of self-worth. Fourth, many of them were seekers; indeed, most of them were some of the time. They were asking religious questions, often profound religious questions, but in their own language.

Today, due to increasing secularization, we have more people than ever before in our communities who don't know what we are talking about. In the U.S.A. today, we have between 120 million and 160 million functionally secular people—which would make the U.S.A. the largest mission field in the western hemisphere, and the third largest on earth. This "domestic mission field" is increasingly receptive; many communities are biblical "harvests."

However, 80 percent of the churches to whom this harvest is entrusted are stagnant or declining. Although 20 percent are growing, most grow by "Vatican Roulette," or by receiving transfers from other churches. Less than 1 percent of our 360,000 churches grow substantially by "conversion growth" from the world.

So some of us are daring to believe that, in the next decade, a hundred thousand churches will rediscover their "first love" and their "main business." Peter Drucker, the management guru, is fond of suggesting that leaders of organizations ask two questions: (1) What is our main business? (2) How is business? I am suggesting that our main business is to join the Holy Spirit in providing a positive answer to Jesus' question: "When the Son of Man return, will he find faith upon the earth?"

What would it take to reach, in great numbers, the secular people of our land? What would it take to reach the people who establishment church people have (prematurely) given up on?

Five Questions for a Congregation Considering Radical Outreach

After years of working with many churches, I have discovered five questions that are pivotally important for the traditional churches more or less like Old East Side Church. I have discovered that a congregation probably needs to be able to answer *all five* questions in the *affirmative*; if the church's leaders fudge on even one of the five questions, their church is unlikely to move "from tradition to mission." Their church will, presumably, continue to provide good chaplaincy services for the people in its congregation, but it is unlikely to become a missionary congregation, reaching lost people quite beyond the church's constituency.

1. Do we want to know them? John explains, in chapter 4 of his Gospel, that "Jews do not fraternize with Samaritans" (v. 9). Likewise, most of our Christians do not fraternize with really unchurched people. They often experience the suggestion as "strange" that we are called to follow Jesus who was "the friend of sinners."

2. Are we willing to go where they are? Jesus went to the town of Sychar, to Jacob's well, then to other gathering places in the town. But most churches *avoid* their city's gathering places, where people engage in conversation and look for Life, lest believers be offended, or even "tempted"![9]

3. Are we willing to spend time with them? When Jesus saw how receptive the town's people were, he stayed for two days with the people. As a result, John tells us, "many more believed because of his word" (4:31). Outreach ministry involves scheduled time, and sweat equity. Do we believe that "people matter to God" enough to invest our time for their sakes?

4. Do we want secular and outside-the-establishment people in our churches? Some churches answer yes to the first three questions but hesitate at this one. At least 80 percent of our churches fail ever to reach out to two groups of people: (1) people who are not "refined" enough to feel comfortable in church; people who have never acquired a "church etiquette" need not apply; (2) people whose lifestyles are too different from ours, or whose lives are too "out of control" for us to feel comfortable with them.

5. Are we willing for our church to become their church too? Even more churches hesitate here. As first-century Judaism was glad for Gentiles to adopt Jewish culture, twenty-first-century churches are glad for "outsiders" to become "like us" and do everything "our way"; but the line of people eager to do that is

usually short! As we have seen, a missionary context requires, in at least some services and ministries, that *we* adapt to the style, the language, the aesthetics, and (yes) the music of the people we are called to reach.

Five Approaches to Reaching People Like the Samaritan Woman

The story in John 4 concludes with the Samaritan woman, and many townspeople, responding rather remarkably to Jesus' visit. If, as I have suggested, she points toward the kind of people we now find all around us, it would be useful to know what made it possible for her to respond. Indeed, my interviews with many converts have demonstrated that, essentially, what helped her respond is what helped them respond. So we conclude with five keys for engaging people like her.

1. Jesus began where she was, rather than where he wanted her to be. Years ago, I learned how important this is from British Methodism's Lord Donald Soper, who reached many secular and marginal people through soapbox speaking, and follow-up conversations at London's famous open-air forums—Tower Hill and Speakers' Corner in Hyde Park. Soper often stated his most important strategic principle: "You have to begin where they are, rather than where you'd like them to be." So Jesus began where the Samaritan woman was—her ancestry, her domestic history, her struggles, questions, and issues.

2. Jesus engaged in the ministry of conversation. We saw, in John 1, that Jesus reached Andrew and his friend through an afternoon of conversation. Now, in John 4, we observe Jesus engaging in an extensive wide-ranging conversation, sometimes informative,

sometimes personal. The woman experienced what Reuel L. Howe would one day call "the miracle of dialogue."[10]

3. In the conversation, every word Jesus used was within her recognition vocabulary; he spoke her language. John 4 is devoid of the esoteric academic language of theologians, and the jargon of the ecclesiastical traditions. Furthermore, in referring to their shared experience at Jacob's well with the metaphor of "living water," Jesus shows the wisdom of employing analogies the people can understand.

4. Jesus treated her with respect. With her shady past and marginal social status, she experienced profound respect from this man. Almost twenty centuries later, we are beginning to discover the redemptive power of respect. For instance, the Hazelden Foundation became clear in the 1960s—as they developed a philosophy of treatment for addictive people—that "the successful treatment of alcoholism requires an environment in which the alcoholic is treated with dignity and respect."[11] George Bernard Shaw's *Pygmalion* features the efforts of linguist Henry Higgins who, with his colleague, Colonel Pickering, persists in engineering a significant set of changes—from flower peddler to duchess—in the life of Eliza Doolittle. Near the play's conclusion, Eliza reflects upon her changed life and attributes the change much more to Pickering than Higgins: "The difference between a lady and a flower girl is how she is treated."

5. Jesus listened, responded, and related to the Samaritan woman with understanding. Following their conversation, the woman invited the townspeople to "come and see a man who told me everything I have ever done! He cannot be the Messiah, can he?" (John 4:29). Jesus had not actually told her everything she had ever done; there hadn't been enough time!

She was displaying the exuberance and hyperbole we typically observe in people who have begun to experience the grace of God. Essentially, she was saying, "Come and meet a man who understands me. Can he be the Messiah?" The Celtic Christian movement would rediscover, four centuries later, that if we make the effort to understand people, they may risk believing that God understands them, too.

Communicating in Many Ways, Especially Through Conversation

The church is "commissioned" to communicate the meaning of the gospel to the entire human race, including people who are beyond the constituencies and fringes of our churches and including people who view life and the world differently than Christians do, who live their lives by values that contrast with Christianity's values of faith, hope, love, and justice. Sometimes, the churches have denied their main business and failed to reach out farther. Sometimes, the churches have accepted the challenge but have expected too few people to carry out the mission (most often, clergy, missionaries, and other professionals) and have expected one way of communicating to do the job (most often preaching, but sometimes Scripture translation and distribution, sometimes ministries of service and "presence").

The most prolific periods of the gospel's spread however have been characterized by its communication in multiple ways. The gospel has been communicated through *languages*—not just through the Aramaic Hebrew of Jesus' people, or the *koine* Greek of Paul's world, or the Latin long favored by the Roman Catholic Church, or even through the English that many North American churches now assume is intelligible to everyone; but through several thousand indigenous languages and dialects. (We saw in chapter 3 that, in addition to language, other "symbol systems" within a culture—such as time and space—also communicate volumes.) The gospel has been communicated *orally*—through conversing, storytelling, teaching, testifying, and (of course) preaching, each done in many different ways, by different personalities, appropriate to different times and cultures. The gospel, since Gutenberg invented the printing press, has been communicated *in print*—through tracts, pamphlets, essays, poems, novels, newspapers, magazines, commentaries, and (especially) the printed Scriptures.

The gospel has been communicated through *music*, not only through Gregorian chants and works such as Handel's *Messiah* and Bach's *Requiem*, but also through thousands of indigenous music forms. The gospel has been communicated through the *visual arts*, from the icons of Eastern Orthodoxy and the frescoes and stained glass windows of Western Christianity to many indigenous forms, ranging from the fine arts to the folk arts. The gospel has been performed through the *performing arts*, though the church has seldom taken full advantage of this opportunity. The harnessing of *electricity* has "amplified" the gospel's potential spread—from microphones and public address systems, to radio, film, television, video, and, most recently, the Internet. Moreover, the gospel has always been communicated *nonverbally*, as people have seen evil defeated, "impossible" people restored, or a tax collector and a zealot in Jesus' twelve disciples, or as people have experienced a Christian's credibility or a Christian fellowship's contagion.

Furthermore, the leaders of Christian movements have usually known better than to overrely on any one communication approach because we experience a remarkable synergy when, say, a seeker is reading devotional literature and Luke's Gospel, *and* is memorizing Scripture texts and the Apostle's Creed, *and* is attending small group meetings and corporate worship, *and* is listening to sermons and teaching tapes, *and* is viewing his new icon collection while listening to Christian music, *and* is conversing with several Christian friends and with fellow seekers and within himself, while he prays each morning and evening and several people pray for him.

Even if one believes in this synergism through which the Holy Spirit moves and which brings a result greater than the sum of the parts, we can still ask which of the ways of communicating the gospel is the most indispensable. The several Christian traditions would usually say that preaching is the most indispensable way. If we affirm that preaching can be done in many settings—from the pulpit to the open air to the television screen—and in many ways, consistent with the medium, the culture, and the preacher's personality, I can almost agree that preaching is the most indispensable way to communicate the gospel. I would place preaching second on the list, however, behind conversation.

Remarkably, conversation is the communication form we engage in the most; we even live in a continual conversation with, and within, ourselves. While we engage in conversation more than any other way of communicating, we think about it the least. The research and literature devoted to understanding conversation is miniscule compared, for instance, to the research and literature devoted to public speaking, mass communication, or music, drama, or film. This has begun to change in recent years.[12]

What is essentially involved in "revelatory conversation"? Conversation in the gospel's service involves listening to the other person, listening for both meaning and feeling, and restating what the person means and reflecting how the person feels—which helps the person to know she or he is understood. So, in part we listen to understand the person. In part we listen that we might speak. Russell Hale used to say that "people can't hear until they have been heard."[13] We also listen to know what to say; as we hear the person's questions and infer what the person needs and where the person is open, we sense what facet of the gospel to share in this conversation and provide one link in the chain that will lead to faith. Being understood is one factor that lowers defenses and makes revelatory conversation possible. The other major factor is trust, and some research indicates that people come to trust us through five factors, the Five C's: (our perceived) commitment, clarity, consistency, caring, and credibility.[14]

Although we should communicate the gospel in as many ways as we can, and we should involve as many people as we can in its communication, conversation is the way that is open to the most Christians and, in synergism with other ways, seems to influence pagans and seekers the most. Many of the great evangelists have also been effective conversationalists.

Take John Wesley, for instance. Since Wesley preached publicly across Britain, traveling 225,000 miles and preaching 40,000 times in a career spanning more than half a century, the Christian tradition remembers Wesley as a preacher. His daily journal reflects just as much as his preaching experiences, however, upon hundreds of his conversations with people in his travels, conversations often continued through his extensive ministry of letter writing. In his time, he was a stimulating and sought-out conversationalist. Samuel Johnson once wrote: "I hate to meet John Wesley; the dog enchants you with his conversation, and then breaks away to go and visit some old woman."

Wesley counseled and prodded his preachers, and other leaders of Methodist societies, to visit with people in their homes and other places. One-to-one conversation (which Wesley sometimes called "close discourse") is the method, he said, to "get within" people, to "suit all our discourse to their several conditions and tempers," and "to choose the fittest subjects." Indeed, Wesley observed that, without conversation, people can hear sermons for years and still not get it. "As great as this labor of private instruction is, it is absolutely necessary. For, after all our preaching, many of our people are almost as ignorant as if they had never heard the gospel. . . . I have found by experience, that one of these has learned more from one hour's close discourse, than from ten years' public preaching."[15]

Old East Side's Enormous Challenge: The "Cultural Enclave"

L et's summarize some of the book's main ideas: The church, in continuity with the early apostles and their churches, is called to reach out and is entrusted with the gospel to give it away. No church is called to serve just its own members or to reach just its inactive members, or the people on the church's fringes, or the other people the church can find who are more or less "like us." In the context of the new "Corinthian" urbanization of North America and Europe, churches are mandated to serve and reach people we have considered in three categories: (1) secular people who have little or no Christian background, (2) the peoples of many tongues and cultures now populating our cities, and (3) the groups of people deemed

195

"hopeless" by establishment people—down-and-outers, up-and-outers, and all the people that no church seems to want.[1] Outreach ministry involves adapting to the needs, the culture, and often the language, dialect, and recognition vocabulary of each target population. It involves serving and communicating in many ways. Supremely, outreach ministry is the privilege of the laity. Our people's assignment, from Jesus Christ, is to penetrate their community as salt and light, as his ambassadors.

On the weekend that I was finishing this book, the Faith and Values section of the local Saturday newspaper carried an Associated Press feature story about the Rev. Jerry Falwell's bold plans to expand his church and college in Lynchburg, Virginia, into a 4,300-acre Christian community. Liberty Village will include a kindergarten, a school, apartment complexes, recreation centers, a golf course, restaurants, shops, and a 1,135-unit retirement center, among other services and ministries. Falwell envisions a day when church members will "never have to leave this place." Liberty Village will serve Christians from "birth to antiquity."[2]

Jerry Falwell's plan for a cradle-to-grave community is only the most recent, and perhaps the largest, of similar projects in churches of many denominational traditions. For three decades or more, some churches in most denominational traditions have been multiplying facilities beyond the traditional sanctuary, offices, and Christian education building; and multiplying on-site ministries, services, and activities for involving their people.

Wonderful ideas sometimes have unintended consequences. I submit that the unintended consequence of this trend is proving to be the de facto creation of "Christian ghettos," which isolate more and more Christians from more and more pre-Christian people. Think about it. Every Christian kid who attends a Christian school is one less Christian kid attending a public school. Every fitness buff who works out at the church's exercise facility is one less Christian befriending people at Gold's Gym. Every couple living in a Liberty Village apartment is one less couple meeting lost people in another Lynchburg apartment complex. The cumulative effect of shifting the location and time of a church's members from the world to the church's campus is enormous. With this trend, more and more school classes, PTA meetings, YWCA facilities, health clubs, apartment buildings, neighborhoods, organizations, and clubs and associations of all kinds, will lack a "critical mass" of Christians; the influence of the remaining nonghettoized Christians will be reduced, and the contacts of pre-Christians with Christians will be fewer and thinner.

Actually, the idea of building large-scale Christian communities is not new; for centuries, medieval parish churches served as the community center for the village people's whole lives. Falwell's dream has more precedent than the Associated Press writer was aware of. It is possible, however, that a good idea in eleventh-century Europe might not be a good idea in twenty-first-century North America. James Russell Lowell once observed that "time makes ancient good uncouth." Likewise, a strategic response to one set of conditions can be a counterproductive response to a very different set of conditions (or to different conditions as perceived).

The medieval church did not understand itself to be in a pagan mission field. Church leaders believed that, following Constantine, they'd built a (more or less) Christian society. In that society, virtually everyone was baptized, and every baptized person was considered a member of the parish; so it made some sense to make the parish church the center of everyone's community life from the cradle to the grave.[3]

We, however, are clear that due to centuries of secularization, churches in North America and Europe find themselves, once again, in an extensive "mission field." We observe, in all of our communities, an increasing number of people with no "Christian memory," who have no idea what Christianity basically claims and offers, who cannot even tell you the name of the church their parents, or grandparents, stayed away from. A smaller percentage of the people in every county in the U.S.A. are regularly involved in a church than a decade ago; a much smaller percentage than a generation ago.

Today, more secular people are open, receptive, or even seeking than at any other time within anyone's memory. Ironically, in the time of an emerging "harvest," more and more churches have retreated into the church and have not been offering what the Christian faith has to offer. Consequently, millions of people have turned to other religions, philosophies, or ideologies—from astrology to Zen, from Communism to Objectivism—to make ultimate sense of their lives; these ways have their own driving values, which shape their people in different ways than Christianity's driving values of "faith, hope, and love" shape Christians.

The burden of this book is to demonstrate that, in this new secular mission field, local churches are called to be missionary congregations. The local church's main business has shifted from chaplaincy to apostolicity. So the main business of Old East Side Church, and Dr. Falwell's Thomas Road Baptist Church, is *not* taking care of "our people," but reaching to people who have not experienced the gospel's power for new life. One hundred and fifty million people in the U.S.A. alone are candidates for forgiveness, justification, second birth, and a purposeful kingdom life. Furthermore, as Paul instructed the Corinthian churches, Old East Side and Thomas Road are both mandated to reach the most "unlikely" people in the community—not only because they matter to God, but also because their changed lives are the greatest of the signs and wonders that draw "regular" people toward the faith.

The problem, from a missionary perspective in any century, is that building a cradle-to-grave community, that Christians will never have to leave, removes them from the real world that matters to God and for which Christ died. At one level, Rev. Falwell acknowledges the potential trade-off: "We have no intentions of building a 'compound'—no wall is going to go up. . . . If a non-Christian family applied, they would be accepted."[4] But what are the odds of that happening? How often would it happen? Is that approach to doing church going to win this world? The difference between building a community essentially for Christians and building a community essentially for serious outreach is enormous.

In any mission field, including ours, the people of God are called and sent to be *in* the world—as salt and light, in ministry and witness—but not to be *of* the world. (The current trend in some mega-churches looks like being *of* the world somewhat more than being *in* the world!) Most traditional congregations, however, are oblivious to the secularization of the Western world, so they do not know why a secular society requires a missionary agenda for churches in the twenty-first century. (In many ways, a majority of churches have not yet adapted to the last third of the *twentieth* century!) Short of a massive paradigm shift, the people of Old East Side Church are not any more likely to move from tradition to mission than they are likely to move en masse to Calcutta. Why is Old East Side stuck? Why is Thomas Road planning to become more like Old East Side? Why are both churches apparently oblivious, or indifferent, to the apostolic opportunity all around? We will reach an explanation by a circuitous route, by way of "globalization." The essay that follows attempts to explain how many traditional churches got into this pattern, and how to shift from tradition to mission.

Globalization is upon us; it is influencing societies

everywhere, including the U.S.A. We observe one expression of increasing globalization as record numbers of American citizens now work overseas—serving, say, their company, a university, or the Peace Corps in another land, another culture, and often in another language.[5] Tragically, however, only about one in seven of these cross-cultural sojourns is satisfying and effective.[6] The other six in seven experience one of two outcomes: (1) Many are so unable to adjust to their new situation that they return home early, without fulfilling their assignment, at significant cost to their organization and at great personal cost. (2) Many others remain technically within the host country, while "retreating" into the "expatriate subculture," in which they, say, play tennis and bridge and share news from home and complain about the nationals and the way they live.

Craig Storti, a popular guru in the field of Intercultural Communication, tells us that both of these patterns—returning home and retreating into an expatriate enclave—are rooted in one's experience of many "cultural incidents" over time.[7] Americans typically expect people of other lands and cultures to be "like us," and therefore to behave "like us."[8] Sometimes, when they are not like us, we find their behavior interesting, even charming. Sometimes, however, when nationals greet an American differently than expected, show up late for a meeting, say yes when they mean no, run a red light, stand too close during a conversation, avoid eye contact during a conversation, withhold their opinions from the class, eat dog meat, sip curdled camels milk, belch after meals, or hire a less-competent cousin (or innumerable other possibilities), this creates a "cultural incident"; the American experiences frustration, rage, or disorientation.

When the American experiences enough of these cultural incidents (without getting in touch with his or her feelings, processing the feelings, and learning from the cultural incidents, *and* without discovering the different culture-based assumptions, attitudes, beliefs, and values behind the confusing behavior of the nationals), he or she has collected enough "brown stamps" to cash them in for an early flight home or a prime-time membership at the Nairobi Hilton Racquet Club. In short, six of seven cross-cultural ventures are unsuccessful because the sojourner never learns to process the cultural incidents, fails to develop an understanding of the host culture, and thus fails to learn to adapt, communicate, and relate with the nationals.

Donald McGavran exposed the fact, a half century ago, that Western missionaries are often as cross-culturally dysfunctional as other sojourners, though they "spiritualize" the decision to leave early and develop their own institutional way to leave without leaving. That institution is called the "mission station," or the "mission compound"—an approach to mission that prevailed in Christian mission's Great Century (1800–1914) and is still the dominant paradigm for doing foreign mission today.

McGavran observed the following pattern. Typically, after an exploratory period in which the pioneering missionaries learn the language, gain rapport with the nationals, and perhaps win a handful of converts, the missionaries take steps to organize their activities within a "mission station," or "compound." They acquire land in a major transportation center, and then they build a chapel, residences for mission personnel and their families, other living quarters for their national helpers, perhaps a school, an orphanage, an agricultural center, a leprosy home, a clinic or hospital, or a printing shop. The church that arises at the compound is a "gathered colony" church, reflecting the missionaries' home culture, composed of the mission personnel and their families and the first converts—who may also live and work at the mission compound, and who often become socially isolated from their people and become more like the missionaries. Most activity takes place within the compound. Mission personnel may engage in forays into the hinterland within manageable travel distance from the compound, establishing casual and cordial contacts with the nationals—but not "living contacts"—and perhaps raising up a few small congregations. The mission station, itself, may or may not have walls around it but, typically, most of the nationals experience themselves estranged from the mission station and what goes on there. When mission leaders discovered how the nationals experienced the mission, they were surprised and shocked; the people had not experienced the mission at all consistent with the mission's good intentions.

McGavran conceded that, typically, mission stations are built as a first stage, with the hope of a later "great ingathering." But, wherever great ingatherings did not occur, the means becomes the end, and mission experiences a diversion to secondary aims. Mission was redefined as education, medicine, relief work, and so on, for which the missionaries could see results, and which involved the activities the missionaries were now used to, which the next generation of missionaries were then recruited to perpetuate. In such an arrangement, the activities of the mission station dominate the mission's agenda; the churches are peripheral, and nationals outside the compound and the churches are incidental—unless they come for an immunization or a literacy class.

So in many lands today, most missionaries who serve the mission's institutions (or, now, the National Church's institutions) are teaching Greek, filling teeth, or checking blood pressure much as they would have back home. In such settings, most missionaries bond with only a few nationals—most of whom have adapted enough to meet the missionaries more than half way—and many missionaries bond with virtually no nationals who are not Christians. Furthermore, as Ralph Winter has observed, your average missionary today is not much more likely to be substantially engaged with an unreached people than are the missionary's supporters back home!

The work in the institutions, and life in the compound, have consumed the time and energies of the missionary, while isolating the missionary enough from the nationals that the cultural incidents are spaced out enough to avoid extensive culture shock and disorientation. Consequently, the missionary never gets around to learning, and adapting to, the host culture. Christianity's apostolic mission to the surrounding mission field is now forgotten, or will come "later." When new missionaries join the mission, they are expected to become creatures of the compound also; anyone who bonds, or even fraternizes too much, with the nationals is suspect. When such missionaries gather to sip tea in the evenings, report news from home, and complain about the nationals, many of them sound much like their fellow citizens at the Nairobi Hilton Racquet Club.

We are now positioned to view Old East Side Church's struggle for a future through a cross-cultural lens. One of the effects of the secularization of the West is the secularization of the cultures of the West. Once upon a time, from the Constantinian era to the Renaissance, the church's beliefs and values pervasively influenced the European cultures from Denmark to Spain; but, today, with some variation from one country to another, and even within the cultural regions of some countries, these cultures now present church people with a constellation of assumptions, attitudes, beliefs, values, behaviors, aesthetics, and lifestyles that is alien to those of the church. Although some Christians may experience temptation in exposure to non-Christian ways, most Christians essentially find those ways to be offensive, and they withdraw.

So, for decades now, Old East Side's people have experienced an endless chain of cultural incidents. In each generation, Old East Side's people have expected non-Christians to believe and live like Christians; when they discovered that the natives were different after all, they were confused or offended. A hundred and fifty years ago, they experienced the frontier towns' saloons, painted women, and gunslingers as confusing or offensive; later, they experienced the sights, the new peoples, and the choices pervading their cities as confusing or offensive. In the 1950s, they felt assaulted by the sudden emergence of rock music, by Elvis's gyrating hips, and by the presence and propaganda of other religions, philosophies, and ideologies. Today, they are put off by what they have heard about unchurched people's clothing and cussing and cohabiting, their divorce and drug habits, their tattoos and taste in music. Many of Old East Side's people have withdrawn from the wider community—lest they be exposed to an immodest woman, a homeless person, a thief, an atheist, a Muslim, a drug transaction, or a New Age bookshop.

Historically, church leaders experienced one cultural incident after another and—not knowing how to own and process their feelings, or how to "exegete" the changing culture around them—they launched a strategy of "retreat." Churches developed more and more ways to "circle the wagons" by developing Christian expatriate subcultures in a fallen society. In the nineteenth century, for instance, we founded most of our colleges in towns far away from the glitter and alternatives of the secular cities.

This tendency to withdraw into enclaves we think we can control has continued since the nineteenth century and has accelerated. We started more Christian colleges to educate our young people, and then Christian schools to educate our kids. We located to Christian neighborhoods near our churches of choice. Our churches organized basketball and softball teams and competed in church leagues. Today, regional churches are building their own activity centers, gymnasiums, and health clubs. Today, the churches and the Christian Yellow Pages coach Christian people to buy their shoes, their car, or their home from Christians; or get their dental work or income taxes done by Christians; or to sign up for their West Indies cruise with a Christian company and travel in the company of other Christians, only. The process expands informally; in their company life, Christians go to lunch with one another, and, in their wider social lives, more and more Christians fill their "dance cards" with the names of Christians only. Then, in our last years, we relocate to retirement communities and nursing homes for Christians. Jerry Falwell's planned "birth to antiquity" Christian village is merely one tip of an extensive iceberg.

By the cumulative effect of those, and many other, withdrawals from cultural incidents, the churches once called to be *in* the world but not *of* the world are no longer in the world that matters to God, no longer loving and befriending pagans. In many Christian settings, being separate from the world is now assumed to be normal Christianity, and complaining about the awful natives and how they behave and live is the indoor sport of choice. As a consequence of these (and many more) retreats into Christian expatriate subcultures, more and more organizations and public institutions lack a critical mass of Christians who are present as salt and light, and more and more pre-Christian people have fewer and fewer confessing Christians in their friendship network.

The widespread use of the Alpha course has exposed the "cultural island" that many churches have become. The Alpha course is the most useful programmatic approach to reaching outsiders that has surfaced in at least a generation. Through a ten-week process, the church offers a combination of hospitality, instruction, celebrative worship, prayer, conversation, friendship, and time that God can use to help many people discover the gift of faith. Many churches adopt the Alpha course; and many of the members take it, believe in it, and are enthused to invite pre-Christian people to the next Alpha course. Then, they discover that most of the church's loyal members do not know enough pre-Christian people well enough to implement the strategy!

That is why Old East Side's problem is more serious, and more complex, than its leaders have known. A new motto or logo, a new program, a new website, or a change of pastors is not likely to fix this problem. Nothing less than a serious paradigm shift—through which they discover their identity as a missionary congregation—will do it, and I think we have learned that Old East Side's people will never experience the paradigm shift inside the walls of the church; but they may well experience it outside the walls—in one (or more) of three ways:

1. They can discover it out in their community. If a cadre of Old East Side's people will expend the sweat equity to get to know lost people, understand them and their culture, and identify with them, ideas for outreach ministries will be entrusted to them. In time the church, say, would be reaching people through a range of classes for literacy, parenting, money management, or English as a second language. The church would reach other people through, say, support groups, recovery groups, and worship services for Spanish-, Tagalog-, Haitian-, and Samoan-speaking people.
2. They can discover it from another church that is already practicing the mission paradigm. As people spend time at the teaching event of a church like Willow Creek that is achieving what Old East Side could achieve, and as they study what this church did and meet its converts and celebrate with its people, they typically catch the vision for what could happen back home.
3. They can discover it cross-culturally through a liminal experience in another part of the world. Something remarkable typically happens in people who, with a

team, spend three weeks building a one-room school-house and worshiping with the indigenous believers in a squatter community on the outskirts of La Paz, Bolivia. As they do no harm, and a little good, they discover who they are, and they contract "apostolic fever." When they return home, they now perceive opportunity for mission in their city they never saw before, and they support world mission more extravagantly than before.

However it happens, *if* the people of Old East Side Church discover who they are, fall in love with the world again, identify with struggling people, and believe in what lost people can become by the grace of God, then even Old East Side will become a contagious movement and the kind of church against which the gates of hell and the powers of death cannot prevail.

If, of course, is the operative word. Ever since God commissioned Jonah to offer grace to the Ninevites, the people of God have (very) often resisted radical outreach to the lost, "different from us," "hopeless" "Ninevites" in their communities. Nevertheless, the High God revealed in Jesus Christ still believes in Old East Side, and he calls the church to become a contagious and redemptive power once again.

Notes

1. Western Christianity's "Corinthian" Future

1. As we shall see in chapter 2, no significant Christian outreach to rural peoples took place before the mission of St. Martin of Tours in the fourth century.

2. See Helmut Thielicke, *The Trouble with the Church: A Call for Renewal*, trans. John W. Doberstein (New York: Harper & Row, 1965).

3. Ron Crandall, *The Contagious Witness: Exploring Christian Conversion* (Nashville: Abingdon Press, 1999).

4. Charles Grandison Finney, *Lectures on Revivals of Religion*, ed. William G. McLoughlin (Cambridge, Mass.: Harvard University Press, 1960), chap. 10.

5. George G. Hunter III, *To Spread the Power: Church Growth in the Wesleyan Spirit* (Nashville: Abingdon Press, 1987), 109.

6. This ancient pattern is returning with a vengeance. See Art Beals, *When the Saints Go Marching Out!: Mobilizing the Church for Mission* (Louisville, Ky.: Geneva Press, 2001).

7. Stanley Ayling, *John Wesley* (Nashville: Abingdon Press, 1982), 158.

2. A Short History of "Apostolic Ministry"

1. Thomas Cahill, *Desire of the Everlasting Hills: The World Before and After Jesus* (New York: Random House, 1999), 78,

2. Carl E. Braaten, *The Apostolic Imperative: Nature and Aim of the Church's Mission and Ministry* (Minneapolis: Augsburg Fortress Press, 1985), 126.

3. David L. Bartlett, *Ministry in the New Testament* (Minneapolis: Augsburg Fortress Press, 1993), 195.

4. Quoted in Adolph von Harnack, *The Mission and Expansion of Christianity in the First Three Centuries,* trans. James Moffatt (New York: Harper & Bros., 1962), 11.

5. See Rodney Stark's summary in *The Rise of Christianity: A Sociologist Reconsiders History* (Princeton: Princeton University Press, 1996), chap. 2, for the near-consensus now achieved by historians and by sociologists such as Stark. It seems that early Christianity reached people in all the classes, not only or primarily the lowest class, and the movement's ranks included people of means and influence.

6. Robert J. Scudieri, *The Apostolic Church: One, Holy, Catholic, and Missionary* (Chino, Calif.: Lutheran Society for Missiology, 1997), 25. Scudieri's book, generally, is a very useful study. The misunderstanding that the faith spreads primarily through preaching is so widespread, and ingrained, that even Scudieri did not transcend it.

7. For my more recent grounding in Acts, I am indebted to Ben Witherington III, *The Acts of the Apostles: A Socio-Rhetorical Commentary* (Grand Rapids, Mich.: William B. Eerdmans Publishing Company, 1998). The space allowed in this part of the chapter does not permit me to do full justice to the range of either Luke's or Witherington's insights for apostolic ministry. My time with his commentary stimulated my own reflection, insights, and conclusions. He is not, of course, to be blamed for anything I have written!

8. The Scots do not (usually) claim Andrew as their apostle; Columba and his apostolic team took Christianity to the Picts of Scotland in the sixth century. The Scots believe that some of Andrew's bones and relics were brought to Scotland in the eighth century.

9. William Barclay, *The Master's Men* (New York: Abingdon Press, 1959), 37-38.

10. Richard Fletcher, *The Barbarian Conversion: From Paganism to Christianity* (Berkeley, Calif.: University of California Press, 1997), 16.

11. Richard Fletcher (Ibid., 34ff.) cites an earlier case of Gregory of Pontus who served a rural pastorate in a town named Neocaesarea beginning about A.D. 240. Fletcher sees Gregory as Christianity's first rural missionary, but this is a stretch; Gregory, following his divinity

studies with Origen, simply returned to his hometown and thus was not functioning as a cross-cultural missionary. Fletcher also sees Gregory's work as the first "rural mission," but, although Gregory's church grew, the ministry produced no wider Christian movement beyond the town he served.

12. Ibid., 42.

13. For a more complete explanation for why the Romans considered many peoples, particularly the Irish "barbarians," see George G. Hunter III, *The Celtic Way of Evangelism: How Christianity Can Reach the West . . . Again* (Nashville: Abingdon Press, 2000), chap. 1.

14. E. A. Thompson, *The Visigoths in the Time of Ulfila* (Oxford: Clarendon Press, 1966), xvii.

15. For a much more complete explanation of the mission of Celtic Christianity, see *The Celtic Way of Evangelism*.

16. Quoted in Fletcher, *The Barbarian Conversion*, 1.

17. Thomas Jackson, *The Works of Rev. John Wesley*, 3d ed., 14 vols. (Grand Rapids, Mich.: Baker Book House, 1979), 1:436-37.

18. Quoted in George G. Hunter III, *To Spread the Power: Church Growth in the Wesleyan Spirit* (Nashville: Abingdon Press, 1987), 52.

19. Harvey Cox, *Fire from Heaven: The Rise of Pentecostal Spirituality and the Reshaping of Religion in the Twenty-first Century* (Reading, Mass.: Addison-Wesley Publishing Co., 1995), 23-24.

20. Two of the most authoritative sources are David Martin, *Tongues of Fire: The Explosion of Protestantism in Latin America* (Cambridge, Mass.: Basil Blackwell, 1990), and Walter J. Hollenweger, *Pentecostalism: Origins and Developments Worldwide* (Peabody, Mass.: Hendrickson Publishers, 1997).

21. Mrs. Howard [Mary Geraldine Guinness] Taylor, *Borden of Yale* (1926; rev. 1952).

3. Apostolic Ministry Through "Cultural Relevance"

1. The reader, understandably, may take issue with me for citing a study I can no longer cite! Or for citing such old data! I sympathize, and can only say the following in my defense: If the Episcopalians were practicing more radical outreach than a generation ago, I think I would have heard something about it by now!

2. See George G. Hunter III, *How to Reach Secular People* (Nashville: Abingdon Press, 1992).

3. Rodney Stark, "Efforts to Christianize Europe, 400–2000," *Journal of Contemporary Religion* 16, no. 1 (2001): 118.

4. I address these features of the "apostolic congregation," and others, in greater detail in *Church for the Unchurched* (Nashville: Abingdon Press, 1996).

5. Ibid., 58.

6. Craig Storti, *Figuring Foreigners Out: A Practical Guide* (Yarmouth, Me.: Intercultural Press, 1999), 5.

7. Ibid., 5.

8. A few major cultures, such as those of Japan and Israel, appear not to fit neatly within a larger macro-culture. A few major cultures fit into one macro-culture or another, depending on who is doing the defining! Is Romanian culture, for instance, within the Eastern European or the Latin European macro-culture?

9. Hall's ideas are expressed in extensive writings, but especially in *The Silent Language* (Garden City, N.Y.: Doubleday, 1959), *The Hidden Dimension* (Garden City, N.Y.: Doubleday, 1966), and *Beyond Culture* (Garden City, N.Y.: Doubleday, 1966).

10. Charles H. Kraft, *Christianity in Culture: A Study in Dynamic Biblical Theologizing in Cross-Cultural Perspective* (Maryknoll, N.Y.: Orbis Books, 1979), 135.

11. Ibid., 65. Originally in Louis J. Luzbetak, *The Church and Cultures* (Techny, Ill.: Divine Word Publications, 1963), 139.

12. Vincent J. Donovan, *The Church in the Midst of Creation* (Maryknoll, N.Y. Orbis Books, 1989), 19.

13. Ibid., 19.

14. Ibid., 20.

15. George G. Hunter III, *The Celtic Way of Evangelism: How Christianity Can Reach the West . . . Again* (Nashville: Abingdon Press, 2000), 41.

16. See my book *The Celtic Way of Evangelism* for a much more complete description and analysis of the apostolic achievement, and the enduring lessons, of the Celtic Christian movement.

17. See my book *To Spread the Power: Church Growth in the Wesleyan Spirit* (Nashville: Abingdon Press, 1987), especially 53-56, for a fuller delineation of early Methodism's cultural awareness and adaptation. The Church of England did become educable—later. When its leaders observed the heroic work of William Booth's Salvation Army among England's urban poor, they created "The Church Army" to help serve these same populations, and, today, much of the world Anglican mission enterprise seems culturally informed.

18. R. Pierce Beaver, "The History of Mission Strategy," in *Perspectives on the World Christian Movement: A Reader*, rev. ed., ed. Ralph D. Winter and Steven C. Hawthorne (Pasadena, Calif.: William Carey Library, 1992), B-62.

19. Harvey Cox, *Fire from Heaven: The Rise of Pentecostal Spirituality and the Reshaping of Religion in the Twenty-first Century* (Reading, Mass.: Addison-Wesley Publishing Co., 1995), 101-2.

20. Ibid., 142-43.

4. Apostolic Ministry Through an Empowered Laity

1. David L. Bartlett observes that "foreshadowings of ordination in the Pastoral Epistles," certain images and "offices" mentioned in those epistles, were used by the later Tradition in developing doctrine(s) of Ordination. Bartlett comments, however, that "The New Testament's most structured view of ministry, foreshadowed in Acts 20 and delineated in the Pastorals, was still more charismatic than the ministerial leadership of most contemporary Assembly of God churches. There were fewer hoops to jump through, fewer authorities to please, fewer professional standards." See *Ministry in the New Testament* (Minneapolis: Fortress Press, 1993), 188, chap. 6.

2. Richard Fletcher, *The Barbarian Conversion: From Paganism to Christianity* (Berkeley, Calif.: University of California Press, 1997).

3. Ibid., 1.

4. Ibid., 85-86.

5. My problem with the historians' "seepage" metaphor is twofold: First, it masquerades as an explanation; but the metaphor is devoid of explanatory power. Second, it suggests that, if a missionary priest is not present, the faith might spread by some mysterious, rather mechanical, process—a process in which Christians are accessories; evangelism, however, is typically a very intentional ministry of a Christian, or (more usually) Christians, to people.

6. Fletcher, *Barbarian Conversion*, 236.

7. My book *The Celtic Way of Evangelism: How Christianity Can Reach the West . . . Again* (Nashville: Abingdon Press, 2000) describes this movement and emphasizes what the ancient Celts can teach us about reaching the "new barbarians" who increasingly populate the cities of the Western world.

8. Richard Baxter, *The Reformed Pastor*, ed. William Brown (Carlisle, Pa.: The Banner of Truth Trust, 1974).

9. Ibid., 12.

10. George G. Hunter III, *Church for the Unchurched* (Nashville: Abingdon Press, 1996), 122-23.

11. This, I regret to report, includes the seminary where I have taught for nineteen years—Asbury Theological Seminary—which thinks of itself as a Wesleyan seminary. Asbury functions, however, more like a reformed seminary with Wesleyan theological opinions. Our predominant theological perspective is Wesley's, but our curriculum is shaped to produce chaplains for church members. Our paradigm for ministry reflects the assumption that the medieval church and Baxter got ministry right and Wesley got it wrong!

12. For more information about SHAPE resources, visit www. pastors.com

13. Art Beals, *When the Saints Go Marching Out: Mobilizing the Church for Mission* (Louisville, Ky.: Geneva Press, 2001).

14. Mel Steinbron, *The Lay-driven Church* (Ventura, Calif.: Regal Books, 1997).

15. Leroy T. Howe, *A Pastor in Every Pew: Equipping Laity for Pastoral Care* (Valley Forge, Pa.: Judson Press, 2000).

16. Ibid., x.

17. Harvey Cox, *Fire from Heaven: The Rise of Pentecostal Spirituality and the Reshaping of Religion in the Twenty-first Century* (Reading, Mass.: Addison-Wesley Publishing Co., 1995), 14-15.

18. David Martin, *Pentecostalism: The World Their Parish* (Oxford, U.K.: Blackwell Publishers, 2002).

19. Hans Küng, *The Catholic Church: A Short History,* trans. John Bowden (New York: Modern Library, 2001), 21.

20. Catechism of the Catholic Church (New York: Doubleday, 1995), 249.

21. Paul Wilkes, *Excellent Catholic Parishes: The Guide to the Best Places and Practices* (New York: Paulist Press, 2001), 63, 65-66. Chapter 4 of Wilkes's book (pp. 57-72) presents a case study on Holy Family.

22. See Hunter, *The Celtic Way of Evangelism,* especially chap. 4.

23. See George G. Hunter III, *To Spread the Power: Church Growth in the Wesleyan Spirit* (Nashville: Abingdon Press, 1987).

24. See George G. Hunter III, *Leading and Managing a Growing Church* (Nashville: Abingdon Press, 2000), 13-14.

25. Address to the Academy for Evangelism in Theological Education, Asbury Theological Seminary, 9 October 1996.

5. Recovery Ministries As a Prototype for Outreach Ministries

1. See George G. Hunter III, *How to Reach Secular People* (Nashville: Abingdon Press, 1992).

2. George G. Hunter III, *The Celtic Way of Evangelism: How Christianity Can Reach the West . . . Again* (Nashville: Abingdon Press, 2000), 100.

3. See "Addiction and Mental Illness" in the April 2000 Research Update of the Hazelden Institute's Butler Center for Research. This study reports that approximately 16 percent of the people *currently alive* are addicted. Since addicted people who do not get into recovery die years sooner than the nonaddicted population, the percentage of people who become addicted must approach 20 percent.

4. See "For Some, Appeal of Addiction Is Embedded in Genetic Code," *Lexington Herald Leader* (10 December 2000). That estimate is probably excessive, but if we include the people whose life is out of control around food, sex, or gambling, the percentage might exceed 25 percent.

5. See Norman Miller, M.D., and Doug Toft, *The Disease Concept of Alcoholism and Other Drug Addiction* (Hazelden, 1990) for a thorough discussion of the "disease" theory of addiction.

6. *Alcoholics Anonymous: The Story of How Many Thousands of Men and Women Have Recovered from Alcoholism*, 4th ed. (New York: Alcoholics Anonymous World Services, Inc., 2001), 58-59.

7. Elizabeth Connell Henderson, a physician, presents a state-of-the-art discussion of these matters, drawing from many studies, in *Understanding Addiction* (Jackson, Miss.: University Press of Mississippi, 2000). See, especially, chapter 2—"Who Gets Addicted and How"—and chapter 3—"The Addicted Brain." Her contrasting profiles (p. 24) of the Type I alcoholic (onset after age 25) and the Type II alcoholic (onset before age 25) are especially useful for ministry leaders.

8. *Lexington Herald Leader* (10 December 2000).

9. "Downer's Downfall," *Time* (11 December 2000): 97.

10. Although the recovery movement's people widely regard personality as a factor in addiction, some scientists have been unable to demonstrate the connection as causal; they suggest that the addictive experience may cause the kinds of personality changes reflected in the following profile. The research of Dr. Henri Begleiter, however, has concluded that many people whose central nervous systems display a "hyperexcitability" are especially vulnerable to addiction; he attributes this trait to distinct brain wave patterns that appear to be inherited. See Doug Toft, "Addiction: A Brain Disease with Biological Underpinnings," *Hazelden Voice* (Winter 2002), 1.

11. William L. White, *Pathways from the Culture of Addiction to the Culture of Recovery*, 2d ed. (Center City, Minn.: Hazelden, 1996). In *The Celtic Way of Evangelism* (pp. 101-3), I reported some of these same insights from White's book.

12. White, *Pathways*, 59.

13. Ibid., 54.

14. Most educated people in the West have been influenced by the "Natural Religion" philosophy of the European Enlightenment which taught that, deep down, all religions are essentially the same. Today, the academic study of religions now demonstrates the opposite—that each major religious tradition has a distinct view of Ultimate Reality, that the Traditions represent dissimilar, mutually incompatible, worldviews. Never mind, most "educated" people are still scripted by the

Enlightenment; indeed, many professors of religious studies still hope to discover that all religions are the same after all! At this point, our knowledge of the culture of addiction that functions, in part, as a religion—with the drug tribe as church, with some members in priestly roles, with the drug as the religion's Idol, and the high as counterfeit religious experience, permits us to look afresh at the big issue of "other religions." Addiction-as-religion gives us one clear case of a very widespread "religious" approach to connecting with Reality that, at its core, is NOT "essentially the same" as Christianity, is essentially delusional and destructive to the human soul, from which Christian experience can liberate its victims. If we grant that, we might find some other religions that, at their core, are delusional and destructive or otherwise pathological. What is the likelihood, mathematically, that the "god" of the addictive culture's religion is the only identifiable idol on earth?

15. Toft, "Addiction."

16. Everyone who works with addicts, or has even known some over time, notices their "arrested emotional development." A popular riddle in the recovery community asks, "What is the difference between a government bond and a drunk?" The answer is, "The bond will mature!" In recovery, people typically work through adolescent emotional issues that nonaddicted people negotiated years ago.

17. Dave Draper, *Brother Iron, Sister Steel: A Bodybuilder's Book* (Santa Cruz, Calif.: On Target Publications, 2001), 27.

18. See Abraham J. Twerski, *Addictive Thinking: Understanding Self-Deception* (Center City, Minn.: Hazelden, 1997).

19. Church leaders who are aware of this typical recovery sequence will, therefore, know to exercise patience in ministering with people in recovery; with the addictive population, one can evangelize "too soon"!

20. This history is reported in William L. White, *Slaying the Dragon: The History of Addiction Treatment and Recovery in America* (Bloomington, Ill.: Chestnut Health Systems/Lighthouse Institute, 1998). Many people regard Ernest Kurtz's *Not-God: A History of Alcoholics Anonymous* (Center City, Minn., Hazelden Educational Services, 1979) as the definitive interpretive history.

21. Bill and Bob still tell their stories in the new edition of the movement's basic text, *Alcoholics Anonymous*, pp. 1-16 and 171-81.

22. Data from Alcoholics Anonymous website, www.aa.org, from January 28, 2002.

23. The scriptural roots for early AA and the Twelve Steps are explained in Dick B., *The Good Book and the Big Book: A.A.'s Roots in the Bible* (Kihei, Hi.: Paradise Research Publications, 1997), especially chapter 4. Dick B. also demonstrates that the reflection of early AA leaders was immersed in the writings of the popular biblically rooted authors of

the period—including Sam Shoemaker, Oswald Chambers, Harry Emerson Fosdick, and E. Stanley Jones.

24. *Alcoholics Anonymous,* 59-60. The Twelve Steps are reprinted with permission of Alcoholics Anonymous World Services, Inc. (A.A.W.S.) Permission to reprint the Twelve Steps does not mean that A.A.W.S. has reviewed or approved the contents of this publication, or that A.A.W. S. necessarily agrees with the views expressed herein. A.A. is a program of recovery from alcoholism *only*—use of the Twelve Steps in connection with programs and activities which are patterned after A.A., but which address other problems, or in any other non-A.A. context, does not imply otherwise. Although Alcoholics Anonymous is a spiritual program, A.A. is not a religious program, and use of A.A. material in the present connection does not imply A.A.'s affiliation with, or endorsement of, any sect, denomination, or specific religious belief.

25. Ibid., 58.

26. For the complete story, see Damian McElrath, *Hazelden: A Spiritual Odyssey* (Hazelden Foundation, 1987). A legend, purportedly accounting for the foundation's name, places that first meeting in "Hazel's Den" at the farmhouse. John MacDougall informs me, however, that the farmhouse had no den! Hazelden is probably named for the farmer's daughter, Hazel Powers.

27. One section of the first edition of the World Christian Encyclopedia features the indigenous names for God in nine hundred of the world's languages—which the Church, historically, adopted and filled with Christian meaning. (See "Names for God in 900 Languages" in *The World Christian Encyclopedia,* ed. David B. Barrett [Oxford and New York: Oxford University Press, 1982], 984-87.) In Greek, He was *Theos,* in Latin *Deus.* In Spanish today, He is *Dios,* in French *Dieu,* in Italian *Dio,* in Brazilian Portuguese *Deus.* In English and Dutch, He is *God,* but *Gott* in German, *Bog* in Russian, and *Gud* in Danish, Norwegian, and Swedish. (But Danes, Norwegians, and Swedes each pronounce "Gud" differently, and the fact that the Church in that region adopted "Gud" rather than "Thor"—the other indigenous option—reflects the strategic choice of the name most useful to the Christian revelation.) Most often, the church in a given linguistic culture has retained their name for the "High God" in the people's former folk religion—while, over time, attaching Christian meanings to the old Name. (Christianity has not always adopted an indigenous name for the High God or the High Power. In Korea, for instance, Protestant missionaries adopted the name *Hamanim,* but Catholic missionaries did not—which may partly account for Protestant Christianity's greater expansion among

Koreans.) In Hindi He is *Ishwar;* Massai people refer to Him as *engAi*—derived from their word for "rain" that they pray will come down and bless them. Many Christian churches in Arabic lands refer to God as *Allah!* The Holy One of the biblical revelation seems willing to be addressed by any name that is sufficiently consistent with His transcendence and character. So Christians, I think, have no informed basis for getting "worked up" about AA's reference to the "Higher Power"!

28. For more on this complex subject, see Linda A. Mercadante, *Victims and Sinners: Spiritual Roots of Addiction and Recovery* (Louisville, Ky.: Westminster John Knox Press, 1996).

29. White, *Pathways,* 54-55.

30. See John Baker, *Celebrate Recovery Leader's Guide: A Recovery Program Based on Eight Principles from the Beatitudes* (Grand Rapids, Mich.: Zondervan Publishing House, 1998) for the most complete overview of Saddleback's approach. Saddleback's target population is wider than AA and its spinoff movements. Saddleback invites people with "all types of habits, hurts, and hang-ups." Consequently, only about one of three people attending Celebrate Recovery is dealing with alcohol or drugs; Saddleback probably engages people struggling with sexual addictions better than any church I know. In most urban contexts, I suggest, churches reaching alcoholics and drug addicts need to be more conversant with addiction theory and lore than Saddleback's leaders appear to be, and in clearer alliance with addiction counselors and the recovery community. For more information, visit www. celebraterecovery.com

31. Since anonymity is often important to people in recovery, Christians who are members in one church will often attend recovery meetings in another church. This is one reason many churches in every community need to provide recovery ministries.

32. See George G. Hunter III, *Leading and Managing a Growing Church* (Nashville: Abingdon Press, 2000) for a full explanation of the "management process" necessary for "getting ministry done through other people."

33. See Dick Wills, *Waking to God's Dream: Spiritual Leadership and Church Renewal* (Nashville: Abingdon Press, 1999), 22.

6. First Baptist Church, Leesburg, As a Church for Everyone

1. Donald A. Atkinson and Charles L. Roesel, *Meeting Needs, Sharing Christ: Ministry Evangelism in Today's New Testament Church* (Nashville: LifeWay Press, 1995), 15.

2. Ibid., 86.

3. See ibid., chap. 4.
4. Ibid., 79.

7. Witness Through Ministry, Hospitality, and Conversation

1. I have assumed that every reader has access to a Bible, and so have resisted the temptation to include the two passages within this text. Most readers will want to read the relevant passage before diving into the next two sections.

2. From "Minutes of Several Conversations Between the Rev. Mr. Wesley and Others, from the year 1744, to the year 1789," in *The Works of John Wesley*, 3d ed., ed. Thomas Jackson (Grand Rapids: Baker Book House 1979), 8:300.

3. The opening chapters of John's Gospel feature Jesus in conversation with people who are not yet disciples. In John 1, for instance, following the conversation with Andrew and his friend, Jesus engages Philip and Nathaniel in conversation. In John 3, he engages Nicodemus, and John 4 features a lengthy conversation with a Samaritan woman Jesus met at Jacob's well in Samaria. John is modeling conversation as an indispensable means of engaging pre-discipled people.

4. See Peter L. Berger and Thomas Luckmann, *The Social Construction of Reality: A Treatise in the Sociology of Knowledge* (Garden City, N.Y.: Doubleday & Co., 1966). See, especially, "Maintenance and Transformation of Subjective Reality," on pp. 135-50 and 147-63. "Symbolic Interactionists" also stress the importance of the inner conversation within the self; talking to oneself in a different way is part of conversion. See Herbert Blumer, *Symbolic Interactionism: Perspective and Method* (Berkeley, Calif.: University of California Press, 1969).

5. The definitive secondary source, summarizing the insights of several thousand specific studies, is Everett M. Rogers, *Diffusion of Innovations*, 4th ed. (New York: Free Press, 1995). Rogers's development of the order of the first three stages is: Awareness, Interest, Relevance. For understanding how people adopt the Christian faith, I have reversed the order of the second and third stages, because my interviews with first-generation Christians have revealed that people, typically, become proactively interested in understanding the Christian possibility for their lives *after* they discover its relevance to some aspiration, need, or motive in their lives. Several years ago, in a conversation with Everett Rogers, I tested my revision of his order. He responded that his version of the order is only approximate, that the "middle" of the order is where he has observed some variation, and

that my variation for informing Christian evangelism struck him as "fully plausible."

6. See Charles G. Finney, *Lectures on Revivals of Religion*, 6th ed. (New York: Leavitt, Lord & Co., 1835), chap. 10. The four sources are Finney's, but the examples are drawn from my interviews with converts and my studies of apostolic congregations.

7. Finney gave preachers more credit, and laity less credit, for reaching people than our data from converts would warrant today.

8. For an explanation of the process by which the West has been "secularized" and, more recently, has become "post-modern," see my book *How to Reach Secular People* (Nashville: Abingdon Press, 1992), chap. 1; and *Church for the Unchurched* (Nashville: Abingdon Press, 1996), chap. 1.

9. Most churches vastly exaggerate the extent to which non-Christian, even destructive, lifestyles will tempt kingdom people. When we do outreach ministry in teams, however, with preparation and prayer before each evening of ministry, and with processing and prayer in the last minutes of a ministry experience, the temptation is negligible; indeed, Christian people usually become much more deeply rooted in their life of faith and their Christian identity from experience in outreach mission.

10. Reuel L. Howe, *The Miracle of Dialogue* (Greenwich, Conn.: Seabury Press, 1963).

11. William L. White published Hazelden's eleven tenets for treating alcoholics in *Slaying the Dragon: The History of Addiction Treatment and Recovery in America* (Bloomington, Ill.: Chestnut Health Systems/Lighthouse Institute, 1998), 209.

12. Most of the helpful literature focuses on a type of conversation. For instance, Phil Harkins's *Powerful Conversations: How High-Impact Leaders Communicate* (New York: McGraw-Hill, 1999) focuses on conversation within organization leadership. Charles J. Stewart and William B. Cash's *Interviewing: Principles and Practices*, 9th ed. (New York: McGraw-Hill, 1999) focuses on the kinds of conversations that inform the work of journalists, managers, salespeople, and health care providers. Shawn Christopher Shea's *Psychiatric Interviewing: The Art of Understanding*, 2d ed. (Philadelphia: W. B. Saunders Co., 1998) focuses on effective conversation for counselors and therapists. As this is written, the new book *Crucial Conversations: Tools for Talking When Stakes Are High*, by Kerry Patterson, Joseph Grenny, Ron McMillan, and Al Switzer (New York: McGraw-Hill, 2002) is generating wide discussion.

13. J. Russell Hale, *The Unchurched: Who They Are and Why They Stay Away* (San Francisco: Harper & Row, 1980).

14. Phil Harkins's model in "Powerful Conversations and Trust" (chapter 6) features the first four, but, in addition, he emphasizes that

"trust requires living one's own beliefs" (101). We know, on many grounds, that—for Christians engaged in the ministry of witness—credibility is the most essential of the five C's.

15. John Wesley, "Minutes of Several Conversations," in *Works* 8:303.

Postscript: Old East Side's Enormous Challenge: The "Cultural Enclave"

1. Readers familiar with my Church Growth writing may be asking if I have abandoned the Church Growth field's "Homogenous Unit" principle. I have not. Contrary to the impressions of Church Growth's detractors, that principle was never intended as a principle of exclusion, but rather a strategy of inclusion. The people of the effective inclusive church do many things together, while also gathering in small groups, large groups, and congregations based on common language, culture, condition, need, interest, or affinity. The next two sentences in the main text should complete this response.

2. Chris Kahn, "A Falwell Utopia," *Lexington Herald-Leader* (6 July 2002), E-1, 4.

3. *If* one doubts that many of a medieval village's baptized people were, in fact, "Christians" in any meaningful sense, and if one believes that medieval Europe was more of a mission field than the Church's leaders perceived, that would argue against the parish church building a community center *for Christians*, then or now, *or* it would argue for the parish church building a community center for everyone—especially for seekers!

4. "Falwell Utopia," E-4.

5. In 1999, according to http://overseasdigest.com, about 3,785,000 Americans were living overseas, *not counting* military and government personnel and their dependents. This website gives the number of Americans known to be living in each country, in some countries by city. Over 35,000 Americans, for instance, live in Belgium; 20,000 in Costa Rica; 10,000 in Denmark; 47,000 in Ireland; 20,000 in Edinburgh, Scotland; 72,000 in Naples, Italy; and over 8,000 in Pretoria, South Africa.

6. L. Robert Kohls, *Survival Kit for Overseas Living: For Americans Planning to Live and Work Abroad*, 4th ed. (Yarmouth, Me.: Intercultural Press, 2001), 1.

7. Craig Storti, *The Art of Crossing Cultures*, 2d ed. (Yarmouth, Me.: Intercultural Press, 2001), chap. 2.

8. Or, I would add, Americans expect "them" to *want* to be like us and live like us! This version of the assumption, I think, is rooted in the

precedent of nineteenth-century European immigrants to the U.S.A.—who *did* want to "assimilate" and "make it" in their new homeland. Americans, generally, have assumed ever since that "they" want to become "like us," even though the newer immigrants from Latin America and Asia have *not* "melted" at the rate the earlier European-Americans did. Americans often assume that something is "wrong" with a people who do not want to become culturally Anglo.

Index